The Perfections of God
Understanding God's Characteristics

The Bible Teacher's Guide

Gregory Brown

BTG
Publishing

4

Contents

Preface

> And the things you have heard me say in the presence of many witnesses entrust to reliable men who will also be qualified to teach others.
> 2 Timothy 2:2

Paul's words to Timothy still apply to us today. We need to raise up teachers who correctly handle and fearlessly teach the Word of God. It is with this hope in mind that the Bible Teacher's Guide (BTG) series has been created. The BTG series includes both expositional studies and topical studies. This guide will be useful for personal devotions, small groups, and for teachers preparing to share God's Word.

The Perfections of God is a study of God's characteristics including his love, goodness, omnipotence, omnipresence, omniscience, eternality, wrath, sovereignty, and much more. It can be used as a seven to fifteen-week small-group curriculum depending how the leader chooses to divide the introduction and the fourteen characteristics. Every week, the members of the group will read a chapter or more, answer the questions, and come prepared to share in the gathering. Each member's preparation for the small group will enrich the discussion and the learning.

Introduction

What are the characteristics of God? Millard Erickson said this about the characteristics or attributes of God, "When we speak of the attributes of God, we are referring to those qualities of God that constitute what he is, the very characteristics of his nature."[1] Ryrie instead calls God's characteristics, his *perfections* because all of the qualities or attributes of God are perfect.[2] In this study, we will consider God's attributes—his characteristics—his perfections.

In considering God's characteristics, I think a good analogy is looking at a married couple. One of the great things about being married is the ability to get to know one person in an intimate way, potentially, for the rest of life. This growing knowledge enables us to learn how to better serve and love him or her daily.

Similarly, Scripture teaches that we are the bride of Christ, and we will be married to God for all eternity (cf. Eph 5:23, Rev 19:7). Since God is the Bridegroom of the church, we must devote ourselves to knowing him intimately so that we might please him and effectively serve him in this loving union throughout this life and the next.

We can only do this properly if we give ourselves to the discipline of study. We must understand his characteristics—his person, his being, what brings him pleasure, what brings him displeasure, etc. Therefore, we will study his characteristics with the hope of better serving our Heavenly Bridegroom for the rest of eternity.

What are some characteristics of God?

Reflection

1. What are some of God's characteristics?
2. What characteristics do we share with God and which ones do we not?
3. What other questions or thoughts do you have about this section?
4. In what ways can you pray in response? Take a second to pray as the Lord leads.

God Is Spirit

The first characteristic is that God is spirit. Consider what Christ said to the woman at the well: "God is spirit, and his worshipers must worship in spirit and in truth" (John 4:24).

What did Christ mean by "God is spirit"? He meant that the essence of God—his makeup—is immaterial. Jesus said this after his resurrection from the dead in Luke 24:39: "Look at my hands and my feet. It is I myself! Touch me and see; *a ghost does not have flesh and bones, as you see I have"*.

Jesus said a "ghost," or it can be translated "spirit," does not have flesh and bones. In the same way, our God does not have a physical makeup. Yes, Jesus does. But Jesus did not eternally exist as a man. He humbled himself and took the form of man in order to save us from our sins (Phil 2:7). God is spirit.

Anthropomorphisms

Now one might ask, "If God is not material, how come so many Scriptures use illustrations of God having human body parts?" We see this particularly when God revealed his glory to Moses in the Old Testament. Listen to what God said in Exodus 33:22–23:

> When my glory passes by, I will put you in a cleft in the rock and cover you with my hand until I have

passed by. Then *I will remove my hand and you will see my back; but my face must not be seen.*

Did you see that? God talks about himself having a back, hands, and a face. How can this be? This is what we call an *anthropomorphism*. This comes from the Greek words "anthropos," which means "man," and "morphe," which means form. These are times when Scripture talks about God in the form of a man. Why does God speak about himself in these terms? He speaks like this to give us a frame of reference, so that we can better understand him.

How can one describe God in understandable words when nothing on earth is like him? You cannot, so God seeks to give us an understanding by using human points of reference like a hand or body. We see many Scriptures like this. The Psalmist said, "Save us and help us with your right hand" (Psalm 60:5). Similarly, Jesus said this:

> My sheep listen to my voice; I know them, and they follow me. I give them eternal life, and they shall never perish; no one can snatch them out of my hand. My Father, who has given them to me, is greater than all; *no one can snatch them out of my Father's hand.*
> John 10:27-29

Again, these are given to help us relate to and understand God, even though every illustration falls short of his true glory.

I think we get some type of understanding of anthropomorphisms when we consider the illustrations often given to represent the Trinity. I remember being confused about the doctrine of the Trinity while in Sunday school class, along with every other student. Because of this, the teacher described the Trinity by using the illustration of ice melting and becoming water, then evaporating as steam. Another time somebody used the illustration of an egg—the yoke, the white, and the shell representing the Father, the Son, and the Holy Spirit. However, each of these illustrations fails miserably in representing the Trinity. Each member of the Trinity is fully God, operates independently and, yet, are one. It's a paradox. With that said, the illustrations of the Trinity, though they fell far short of the glory of God, were mildly helpful at that young age. Similarly, even though God does not have material form, he uses illustrations we can relate to in order to help us comprehend something of his glory.

The fact that anthropomorphisms are simply points of references is also seen when God uses animal forms to describe himself. Scripture talks about him covering us with his wings like a bird (cf. Psalm 91:4). Does God really have wings? No, he is a spirit, but he wants us to understand that he cares for us like a mother hen cares for her chicks. That's an illustration we can understand even though it still falls miserably short of God's true glory. God's care for us is infinitely greater than any hen could ever possibly care for her chicks.

What else can we learn about God since he is spirit?

Invisible

Because God is spirit, this also means he is "invisible." We cannot see God. This is what John taught in his Gospel. Look at what he said in John 1:18: "No one has ever seen God, but God the One and Only, who is at the Father's side, has made him known." The only human that has ever seen God in his full glory is Jesus, and, therefore, it is through Jesus that we can have a better understanding of God.

However, even though God is invisible, it should be noted that at times in Scripture God chose to take physical form to reveal himself to man in sensible ways. As mentioned previously, these temporary physical manifestations are called theophanies. We saw one of these in the book of Isaiah. Isaiah saw the Lord in physical form. He said this in Isaiah 6:1 "In the year that King Uzziah died, *I saw the Lord seated on a throne, high and exalted, and the train of his robe filled the temple.*"

In addition, God revealed himself throughout biblical history in many different physical forms. He revealed himself in a flame with Moses (Ex 3:2), through a man with Abraham (Gen 18:1-2), through a cloud with Israel (Ex 13:21), through an angel with Gideon (Judges 6:22), etc.

Ultimately, the fullest expression of God has been given in Jesus Christ. This appearance would not be considered a theophany because this appearance was not temporary. Christ will dwell throughout eternity as the God-man (cf. 1 Tim 2:5), and it is through Christ that we can see God. The writer of Hebrews said this:

> *The Son is the radiance of God's glory and the exact representation of his being,* sustaining all things by his powerful word. After he had provided purification for sins, he sat down at the right hand of the Majesty in heaven.
> Hebrews 1:3

Jesus said, "Whoever has seen me has seen the Father" (John 14:9). The ultimate expression of God is seen in Jesus Christ, his Son.

God is spirit, and therefore, he is invisible. However, at times he has chosen to reveal himself to men in theophanies and ultimately through his Son, Jesus Christ.

How can we apply the reality that God is spirit?

Application

What does this mean for us?

When Jesus says, "God is spirit, and his worshipers must worship in spirit and in truth'" (John 4:24), he essentially is saying this reality should affect how we worship him. Since God is spirit, "we must worship God in spirit and in truth" (John 4:24).

What does it mean to worship in spirit? To worship in spirit means to worship with the right heart or the inner man.

In the context, Christ was trying to teach a Samaritan woman that worship is not a matter of being in Jerusalem at the temple or being in Samaria. It is not primarily a matter of where you are or what you are doing, because worship is a matter of the heart. God is spirit, so we must worship him in spirit.

Some have primarily seen this as Christ referring to our need for the Holy Spirit in worship, but most translators do not capitalize the word "spirit" because it has no article behind it. It doesn't say "the Spirit." Worship is primarily a matter of the heart—the inner man. It is not so much about location or activity. You can sing a song and not worship, give an offering and not worship. It is a matter of the inner man; it is a matter of having the right heart.

We see this in the New Testament with the Pharisees. Jesus said, "These people honor me with their lips, but their hearts are far from me. They worship me in vain" (Matthew 15:8). Christ warned his disciples to not worship in the same way the Pharisees did. He said: "Be careful not to do your 'acts of righteousness' before men, to be seen by them. If you do, you will have no reward from your Father in heaven" (Matthew 6:1). When the Pharisees worshiped, their hearts were not in the right place. They gave to be seen by men; they prayed and fasted to be seen by others, and therefore, that was their reward. They did not approach God properly in the inner man. God is spirit, and he must be worshiped with our spirit.

Certainly, it's the same for us. Consider what Paul said about giving in 2 Corinthians 9:7: "Each man should give what he has decided in his heart to give, not reluctantly or under compulsion, for God loves a cheerful giver." Giving weekly or monthly is not the most important aspect; it is the manner of the heart. It must not be reluctant or under compulsion, but out of a joyful heart. Otherwise, it means nothing.

Consider what Paul taught in 1 Corinthians 13:1–3:

> If I speak in the tongues of men and of angels, but have not love, I am only a *resounding gong or a clanging cymbal*. If I have the gift of prophecy and can fathom all mysteries and all knowledge, and if I have a faith that can move mountains, but have not love, I am nothing. If I give all I possess to the poor and surrender my body to the flames, but have not love, I gain nothing.

Paul names all these things that would typically be worship to God. He names speaking in tongues, prophecy, faith, giving everything to the poor, and even being given to the flames as a martyr, but without love—without the right heart—it is nothing to God. It is like a resounding gong or a clanging cymbal.

Much of worship on Sundays is just a bunch of clanging cymbals. Clanging cymbals create a loud noise nobody wants to hear, and there is a lot of that in the church. I have no doubt that many times on Sunday, God is in pain by hearing the worship. He hears a constant clanging because it comes from hearts that are not serious, not contemplative, and not reverent. True worship is a matter of the inner man. It is a matter of the heart, will, and emotions. God is spirit and so we must worship him in spirit.

Understanding that God is spirit should drastically affect our worship. *How can we practically worship in spirit in order to honor God?*

To worship in spirit, with the right heart, means that our worship is universal.

That means everything we do can be worship. It is not localized. It is not only a Sunday thing or about being in a church building. First Corinthians 10:31 says: "So whether you eat or drink or whatever you do, do it all for the glory of God." Paul says our eating, our drinking, and whatever else we do should glorify God.

1. To worship in spirit, with the right heart, means to give God our best.

We saw this throughout the Old Testament. God would never accept anything that was not the best. This is specifically seen in the instructions given for offering a burnt sacrifice. It had to be a lamb without blemish. It had to be the worshiper's best (cf. Malachi 1:6–10) or it would be rejected.

2. To worship in spirit, with the right heart, means that worship must be our priority.

Christ said this in the Beatitudes: "Blessed are the pure in heart, for they will see God" (Matthew 5:8).

The pure in heart has the meaning of being single in mind or focus. It is the single in focus that see God and have his blessing. Their focus—their priority—is knowing God and bringing pleasure to him. Too often, our hearts are divided, and it quenches our worship. David said this: "Teach me your way, O LORD, and I will walk in your truth; *give me an undivided heart, that I may fear your name*" (Psalm 86:11).

3. To worship in spirit, with the right heart, means to be zealous in pursuing God.

Listen to what God said through Jeremiah: "You will seek me and find me when you seek me with all your heart" (Jeremiah 29:13). Worship must involve zeal. The zealous and they alone will find God and receive his blessing. They are like a deer who is desperate for water. It is those he rewards. The casual worshiper receives nothing from God. The Psalmist modeled acceptable worship when he prayed this: "As the deer pants for streams of water, so my soul pants for you, O God. My soul thirsts for God, for the living God. When can I go and meet with God?" (Psalm 42:1–2). True worship must be zealous (cf. Romans 12:11).

4. To worship in spirit, with the right heart, means to worship with holiness.

David said this: "If I had cherished sin in my heart, the Lord would not have listened" (Psalm 66:18). Sin quenches not only our prayer life but also our worship. If I enjoy nurturing my anger towards someone who hurt me, or if I cherish an impure relationship, the Lord will not hear me. If I cherish music so much that I will illegally download it, the Lord will not hear me. Worship must be in holiness.

5. To worship in spirit, with the right heart, means to live peaceably, without division.

Listen to what Christ said in Matthew 5:23–24:

Therefore, if you are *offering your gift at the altar and there remember that your brother has something against you*, leave your gift there in front of the altar. First go and be reconciled to your brother; then come and offer your gift.

Jesus said one should not offer a gift in worship if he is walking in discord with another brother. As much as it depends on us, we must live in peace with our brothers and sisters (Romans 12:18).

The fact that God is spirit should challenge us in our worship. He is looking at the spirit of man, the heart of man, when we approach him for worship (1 Sam 16:7).

Reflection

1. What does God being spirit mean and how should that affect our worship of him (cf. John 4:23)?
2. What other questions or thoughts do you have about this section?

19

3. In what ways can you pray in response? Take a second to pray as the Lord leads.

God Is a Person

As we think about God as spirit, we might be tempted to think that God is not a person. God is a person. Wayne Grudem said this about God's personhood:

> In the teaching of the Bible, God is both *infinite* and *personal*: he is infinite in that he is not subject to any of the limitations of humanity, or of creation in general. He is far greater than everything he has made, far greater than anything else that exists. But he is also personal: he interacts with us as a person, and we can relate to him as persons.[3]

In fact, his personhood may be most clearly seen in the fact that God made man in his image. Listen to Genesis 1:27: "So God created man in his own image, in the image of God he created him; male and female he created them."

Because God made man in his image, we can probably learn a lot about God's person by studying humanity and vice versa. In what ways do we see God's personhood? We see it in the fact that God demonstrates characteristics of personality such as anger, joy, and consciousness. Scripture teaches he is angry at sin all the time (Psalm 7:11). Also, when we are walking in holiness and living the life he has called us to, he rejoices over us and even sings. Zephaniah 3:17 says this:

The LORD your God is with you, he is mighty to save. He will *take great delight in you, he will quiet you with his love, he will rejoice over you with singing.*

Scripture also teaches that he demonstrates the emotion of jealousy. God declares that he is a jealous God who will share his glory with no one. Deuteronomy 6:15 says this: "For the LORD your God, who is among you, is a jealous God and his anger will burn against you, and he will destroy you from the face of the land."

We also see that God demonstrates consciousness. We see this in the fact that he makes decisions. He plans and foreordains things. This is clearly demonstrated in the doctrine of election. God chose people for salvation before time. Ephesians 1:4–5 says this:

For he chose us in him before the creation of the world to be holy and blameless in his sight. In love he predestined us to be adopted as his sons through Jesus Christ, in accordance with his pleasure and will.

As we study the rest of his characteristics, they all in some way demonstrate his personhood. It is because God is a person that we can have an intimate relationship with him.

Applications

How can we apply the personhood of God?

1. His personhood reminds us that we can get to know God more and more as with any person.

Paul prays this in Ephesians 1:17: "I keep asking that the God of our Lord Jesus Christ, the glorious Father, may give you the Spirit of wisdom and revelation, *so that you may know him better.*"

2. His personhood reminds us that we must develop sensitivity to his person.

Scripture says that we can grieve the Holy Spirit (Ephesians 4:30) and quench the Holy Spirit (1 Thessalonians 5:19). Therefore, like with any person, we must develop a sensitivity to God in order to please him in every way.

When a person is in a relationship, often one can tell when their partner or friend is mad even without a word. This is true because that person and has become sensitive to him or her. We must, similarly, develop this sensitivity to God.

Developing sensitivity to God has an objective side. It is developed by studying his Word. By doing this, we learn what does and does not please him. But there is a subjective side as well. At times, we may even sense God's feelings. Jeremiah said this: "But I am full of the wrath of the LORD, and I cannot hold it in" (Jeremiah 6:11).

Jeremiah could feel God's anger at Israel. At times we may feel this as well. We may feel the Spirit of God grieving over a movie we are watching or disobedience in a friend's life. We may feel his love, joy, or peace. Paul said he longed for the Philippians with the very affections of Christ (Phil 1:8). He felt the way Christ felt about them. He had developed sensitivity to his Savior's emotions and so must we.

3. His personhood reminds us that God is not a tool or an object to be used.

What does it mean that God is not a tool? See, a tool is only used for a specific purpose. We use a toothbrush to clean our teeth, but we don't have a relationship with a toothbrush. We only care about it to accomplish our purpose.

Sometimes, people treat one another like this. We network or talk to people only to open potential doors for a job or a promotion. Sometimes, people are willing to step over others or mistreat them to get what they want out of life. This is treating someone like a tool.

Sadly, many Christians treat God like a tool. He is just a genie in a lamp. When they want something, they pray to God. When they go through a trial, they come to him, but when things are okay, they ignore him. They are treating God like a tool, to get what they want, instead of as a person.

God is a person, and he wants to have a relationship with us. He sent his Son to die for this purpose, so we can have eternal life, which is knowing God (John 17:3).

Reflection

1. What does God being a "person" mean? How do we see this reflected in Scripture?
2. What other questions or thoughts do you have about this section?

3. In what ways can you pray in response? Take a second to pray as the Lord leads.

God Is Independent

What does the independence of God mean? It essentially means that God does not need anything. He doesn't need anything to be who he is or contribute to who he is. Tony Evans said this about God's independence:

> This understanding can enhance our worship of God, because while God has a voluntary relationship to everything, He has a necessary relationship to nothing. In other words, God relates to His creation because He chooses to, not because He needs to. For example, if you show up for worship at your church, that's good and God is glad to see you. But He will not be worse off if you stay home. He's not going to panic.[4]

We, on the other hand, are dependent. We are dependent on our parents for life and clothing as children, and when we are older, we are dependent upon friends, family, job, education, etc. In a sense, we need these things to make it in life or society.

But we serve a God who needs nothing because he is independent. Look at what Paul said to the Athenians in Acts 17:24–25:

The God who made the world and everything in it is the Lord of heaven and earth and does not live in temples built by hands. *And he is not served by human hands, as if he needed anything, because he himself gives all men life* and breath and everything else.

Paul says, "He is not served by human hands, as if he needed anything" (v. 25). What does Paul mean by "he is not served by human hands"? Don't people serve God all the time? They serve him at church; they serve him at work; they serve in their personal worship.

Paul means at least two things by saying that God is not served by human hands. First, he simply means that God does not need anything. God is independent. But secondly, he means that God is not served by human hands because he is *the giver*. He says, "because he himself gives all men life and breath and everything else" (v.25). What exactly does that mean?

We may get a good picture of this when small children buy their parent a gift. Did they buy the gift? Yes. But in another sense, the parent bought the gift because it was the parent's money. See, the parents are the ones who make money in the household. Similarly, Paul says we can't really serve him because he has given us all things. Can we really give God money on Sunday if he has already given it to us? In a sense, we can't. We can't because God is independent, and he is the true giver of all things. We can give only because he has given to us.

That is the wonderful thing about God. He doesn't need us, but he allows us and calls us to worship him, though he doesn't need anything.

Created for His Enjoyment

28

Well, one might ask, why did he create us then if he is independent? Was it because he was lonely or bored?

No, not at all. There are many things in life that I don't need. I don't need to look at ESPN to see who won the latest NBA game. That's something I do because I enjoy it. God made us because he enjoys us. Look at what he says about Israel and, through extension, the people of God of all times: "The LORD your God is with you, he is mighty to save. *He will take great delight in you, he will quiet you with his love, he will rejoice over you with singing*" (Zephaniah 3:17).

It says he takes great delight in us and he will rejoice over us with singing. We often see people who are musically talented write or sing songs to people they care about. Our worship songs to God are commonly written this way. However, God also sings over us and delights in us. He delights in us, especially, when we are following him and walking in the unique giftings that he gave us. It brings him pleasure because we are fulfilling his purpose.

Scripture would say our high calling is to bring God both joy and pleasure. Colossians 1:16 says this:

> For by him all things were created: things in heaven and on earth, visible and invisible, whether thrones or powers or rulers or authorities; *all things were created by him and for him.*

All things were made for him—to bring glory to God and to bring him pleasure.

A great illustration of this is seen in the story of Olympic runner, Eric Liddell. In 1924, he was competing in the Olympics and had decided this would be his last competition before he went into full-time missions. One person asked him, why not just stop running now and go into missions? He told the person, "I believe God made me for a purpose, but he also made me fast. And when I run I feel His pleasure."[5]

For each of us, God has given us certain gifts. For some, he made us intelligent, others athletic, others are great with their hands, and others are gifted at serving or teaching. When we do the things that God created us for, he takes great pleasure in us as well.

Creation's Dependence

The other side of God's independence is our dependence on him. Listen again to what Paul said to the Athenians: "And he is not served by human hands, as if he needed anything, *because he himself gives all men life and breath and everything else*" (Acts 17: 25). We need God for everything, even life and breath.

Look at what else Paul says in Colossians 1:17: "He is before all things, and *in him all things hold together*." In talking about Christ, he says that he holds "all things together." This means that not only does he give us life and breath, but he holds the trees, the plants, the oceans, the stars, and all the cosmos together. Everything is dependent upon him; we can do nothing apart from God.

I think we may get a clearer picture of the dependence of man in David's illustration of God being a shepherd in Psalm 23. Listen to Psalm 23:

> *The LORD is my shepherd, I shall not be in want.* He makes me lie down in green pastures, he leads me beside quiet waters, he restores my soul. He guides me in paths of righteousness for his name's sake. Even though I walk through the valley of the

shadow of death, I will fear no evil, for you are with me; your rod and your staff, they comfort me. You prepare a table before me in the presence of my enemies. You anoint my head with oil; my cup overflows. Surely goodness and love will follow me all the days of my life, and I will dwell in the house of the LORD forever.

Sheep are very interesting animals because they can't survive without a shepherd. They can't feed themselves; they can't protect themselves. Other animals can at least run away from predators but not sheep. They will idly stand by until their death. From this we get the phrase, "Like a lamb to the slaughter" (Is 53:7). They are very fearful; one commentator said they are often fearful of running water or the dark. The shepherd must care for them like a baby. The shepherd would protect them with his rod and with his staff he would guide them. They are prone to go astray, and he must constantly bring them back.

Many have wondered if God made these dependent animals just as an illustration of how much humans need God. We are prone to fear: fear about the past, present, and future. We need a shepherd who calms our fear. We cannot direct our lives; we need a shepherd to guide us in the direction to go. We commonly go astray; we need a shepherd to save us from our wandering heart.

Our God is independent, and we are dependent upon him.

Applications

What are some applications we can take from this?

1. Understanding God's independence reminds us of God's love for us.

He didn't need to create us since he doesn't need anything, but God created us because he loves us. Paul believes this is a very important reality for Christians to understand. Look at what he prays in Ephesians 3:17–19:

> And I pray that you, being rooted and established in love, *may have power, together with all the saints, to grasp how wide and long and high and deep is the love of Christ,* and to know this love that surpasses knowledge—*that you may be filled to the measure of all the fullness of God.*

Paul prayed for the saints to know the depth and height of God's love. This is important because knowing that someone loves us will often radically change us. On earth, those who experience the greatest human love get married and spend the rest of their lives serving and getting to know one another.

When we know God's love, it should have a dramatic effect on us as well. Paul said this understanding would lead to our being filled with the "fullness of God." This means we would be controlled and empowered by him (cf. Eph 5:18).

No doubt, this is the reason Satan often attacks the love of God. In the Garden of Eden, Satan essentially was trying to make it seem like God did not really care about Adam and Eve. He said, "Did God really say you couldn't eat of every tree in the Garden?" He tried to make God's commands feel restrictive and domineering instead of loving. Then, he essentially calls God a liar. "You surely won't die if you eat from the tree. Instead, you will be like God."

Satan works overtime to keep us from knowing God's love. He plants doubt, anger, and fear in order to keep us from being transformed by it and saved by it. "For God so loved the world he gave his only begotten son that whosoever believes in him should not perish but have everlasting life" (John 3:16).

Like Paul, we must pray for ourselves and others to have power to grasp God's love so that we may be transformed by it. God's independence reminds us about how much God loves us.

2. Understanding God's independence reminds us of our need to be dependent.

Jesus said in Matthew 18:3 that in order for a person to enter the kingdom of God, they must become like a child. The word "child" in that context is used of a very young child, a toddler or an infant. He was saying that the person who enters the kingdom of God has learned dependence. An infant can't feed himself, clothe himself, guide himself, or protect himself. He is totally dependent upon his parents. In the same way, a person who is saved learns he can do nothing to get into the kingdom of God on his own; he is totally dependent upon God.

However, this is not only true in regards to salvation, but also in sanctification. In the next verse, Christ says he who becomes like this child is greatest in the kingdom of God (Matthew 18:4). The person who learns dependence upon this independent God shall be the greatest in the kingdom of God. This person knows his utter weakness and need for the Almighty.

How much do we need God? We can tell how much we need God by considering how much we pray, read the Bible, worship, or need to be around his people. This shows something of our dependence upon him. Some people can go weeks without reading his Word, which shows their lack of dependence, their lack of childlikeness.

In a very real sense we must learn to develop this. We must learn as a discipline to be like children in order to enter the kingdom. We can do nothing to save ourselves, and therefore, we must put our weight and faith fully on Christ. However, we must also learn this dependence to become great in the kingdom, essentially to grow.

God's independence reminds us of these things. It reminds us of his love for us and our dependence upon him. Let no one doubt how much he loves us, and let no one doubt how much we really need God.

Reflection

1. What does God's independence mean?
2. In what ways are we and all creation dependent upon God, and how should this affect our daily lives?
3. What other questions or thoughts do you have about this section?
4. In what ways can you pray in response? Take a second to pray as the Lord leads.

God Is Immutable

Scripture would also teach that God is immutable. "Immutability means not having the ability to change."[6] This is a very important characteristic of God because it affects all his other characteristics. When we say that God is omniscient, that "he knows all things," it means he will always know all things. When we say he is loving, that means he will always be loving and always act in accordance with his love, even if that includes discipline. *Our God is always the same; he is unchangeable in his character*. Listen to a few texts that describe this:

> In the beginning you laid the foundations of the earth, and the heavens are the work of your hands. They will perish, but you remain; they will all wear out like a garment. Like clothing you will change them and they will be discarded. But you remain the same, and your years will never end.
> Psalm 102:25–27

As David looked at creation, he realized that this present earth and the way it operates will one day pass away. It will wear out like a garment or a piece of clothing and be discarded. But God, he remains the same. He does not corrupt or change; he will live and remain the same throughout eternity.

Listen to what God said through Malachi: "I the LORD do not change" (3:6).

As we look at God, who is unchangeable, this certainly reflects a characteristic which we as humans do not share, for we are always changing. We are always growing in knowledge and wisdom. Our bodies are always changing with age or with every meal, but God never changes.

Sometimes, the fact that we are always changing makes it difficult to understand one another, even in the closest unions such as marriage. How can you really know someone completely if he or she is always changing? "Hold up, I thought you didn't like coffee." "I do now." "What? When did this happen?"

This may make it hard to know or understand one another, but it makes it easier to know God. He is the same yesterday, today, and forever (Hebrews 13:8).

Apparent Changes

God does not change, and therefore, we can trust that he will always act in accordance with his characteristics. Now with this said, some texts would seem to indicate that God changes. Let's look at a few:

> The LORD saw how great man's wickedness on the earth had become, and that every inclination of the thoughts of his heart was only evil all the time. The LORD was grieved that he had made man on the earth, and his heart was filled with pain. So the LORD said, "I will wipe mankind, whom I have created, from the face of the earth—men and animals, and creatures that move along the ground, and birds of the air—for I am grieved that I have made them."
> Genesis 6:5-7

In Genesis 6:6, it says that God was sorry that he made man. The KJV actually says he repented. Doesn't this seem like God changed his mind? He made men, and now, he is going to destroy them.

Certainly, we see God changing his mind, but only in accord with his characteristics. God is a holy God, and because he wants holiness, he will bring discipline or judgment. We see this characteristic throughout Scripture. One time he pronounced judgment on the city of Nineveh in the book of Jonah, and when they repented, he had mercy and removed the judgment (Jonah 3). This does not contradict God's immutability; it is a reflection of it. God is both holy and merciful. He always acts in accord with his characteristics. This is true because he is faithful and cannot deny himself (2 Tim 2:13). He does not change like the shifting shadows (James 1:17).

Unchangeable in Sovereign Plans

Not only is God unchangeable in his person but also in his sovereign plans. Listen to what he said in Psalm 33:11: "But the plans of the LORD stand firm forever, the purposes of his heart through all generations." His sovereign plans stand firm because our Lord does not change in his person and his characteristics. These plans include things like prophecy.

For example, Christ said he is coming back to take his people to himself (John 14:3). God said that in the end times, tremendous wars and natural disasters will occur right before Christ's coming (Matt 24:7, Rev 6:12-13). At his coming, people will be separated from one another and sent either into everlasting punishment or into everlasting life (Matt 25:46). We can trust these prophecies. His immutability means that we can trust the prophecies and plans he has shared with us in Scripture.

Unchangeable in Promises

Not only is God unchanging in his sovereign plans, but he is unchanging in his promises. Listen to what Numbers 23:19 says: "*God is not a man, that he should lie*, nor a son of man, that he should change his mind. Does he speak and then not act? *Does he promise and not fulfill?*"

How can we apply this?

This means we can trust every promise he has in Scripture because he is unchangeable. He is unchangeable in his person, in his plans, and his promises to us.

Does he promise to save you if you put your trust in the Son (Romans 10:13)? Then you can trust him. Does he promise to forgive your sins (1 John 1:9)? He will forgive. Does he promise to guide you throughout life as your shepherd (Psalm 23)? You can trust he will lead and guide you in the right paths because he is unchangeable; he is immutable.

This characteristic of God gives us great comfort. We can trust him because he doesn't change like man does.

Reflection

1. What does God's immutability mean?
2. In what ways does God's immutability comfort you?
3. What other questions or thoughts do you have about this section?
4. In what ways can you pray in response? Take a second to pray as the Lord leads.

God Is Good

Another characteristic of God is the goodness of God. What does the goodness of God mean? Tony Evans said this: "God's goodness can be defined as the collective perfections of His nature and the benevolence of His acts...God is good by nature and good in what He does."[7] Wayne Grudem defines it this way: "The goodness of God means that God is the final standard of good, and that all that God is and does is worthy of approval."[8]

God Is the Standard of Goodness

Essentially, this means that God is good in his nature and everything that he does is good. We see this in how Christ responds to the rich man in Luke 18. The rich man approaches Jesus about how to inherit eternal life and calls Jesus good. Jesus responds with, "Why do you call me good?"..."No one is good—except God alone" (Luke 18:19).

Jesus declares that no one is good except for God alone. Christ says this to help the rich man recognize that Christ was actually God, and therefore, the only way to eternal life. In saying that only God is good, Christ essentially is saying that God is the definition of good. And therefore, it is by looking at God that we can determine if anything is truly good at all. This is very similar to how John declares that God is love (1 John 4:8). We cannot know what love is unless we know God. In the same way, we cannot know what is good unless we compare it to God. As Grudem said, "God is the standard of what is good and everything he does is worthy of approval."

In fact, *Scripture would declare that God's goodness is the sum total of his characteristics.* We see this in the story of Moses asking to see God's glory. Look at what Exodus 33:18–19 says:

> Then Moses said, "*Now show me your glory.*" And the LORD said, "*I will cause all my goodness to pass in front of you,* and I will proclaim my name, the LORD, in your presence. I will have mercy on whom I will have mercy, and I will have compassion on whom I will have compassion.

God tells Moses that he will grant his request to see the LORD's glory. He will do this by causing his "goodness" to pass in front of him. What does God's goodness look like? It is described in Exodus 34:5–7:

> Then the LORD came down in the cloud and stood there with him and proclaimed his name, the LORD. And he passed in front of Moses, proclaiming, "The LORD, the LORD, the compassionate and gracious God, slow to anger, abounding in love and faithfulness, maintaining love to thousands, and forgiving wickedness, rebellion and sin. Yet he does not leave the guilty unpunished; he punishes the children and their children for the sin of the fathers to the third and fourth generation."

The goodness of God is described in verses 6 and 7. It mentions his compassion, his grace, his patience (slow to anger), his love and faithfulness, and even his wrath. Everything that God does is good, and therefore, his goodness can summarize the rest of God's characteristics. We worship a God who is loving, patient, and compassionate simply because he is good. Even his wrath is a reflection of his goodness. Every person God loves, he disciplines (Hebrews 12:6). Everything God does is good.

This truth is a challenge to those who question God's goodness when they consider the many bad things that happen in life. They say, *"Why does God allow bad things if he is good? Why do innocent people die if God is good?"* It should be known that tsunamis, flooding, famine, government corruption, murder, family discord, etc., were never part of God's original plan. God did not create the earth with problems. When he finished his creation, he declared that it was very good (Genesis 1:31). It was not until sin came into the world that the earth developed its current problems. Therefore, the evil in creation must be attributed to someone other than God. He is sovereign and in control of everything, but evil cannot be attributed to him (cf. James 1:13). However, although God is not the author of evil, he nonetheless uses all things, including evil, for his glory.

God Is the Source of Good

> Every good and perfect gift is from above, coming down from the Father of the heavenly lights, who does not change like shifting shadows.
> James 1:17

James says every good and perfect gift comes from above. When we look at family, friends, job, rain, sunshine, etc., they must all be attributed to God. He is the source of everything good. In fact, God gives these perfect gifts even to those who do not love him. Look at what Christ said in Matthew 5:45: "He causes his sun to rise on the evil and the good, and sends rain on the righteous and the unrighteous."

God in his goodness gives rain and sunshine to the evil and good alike. Theologians have called this *common grace*. This is grace that God gives to all people, regardless of whether they accept him or not. Consider Acts 17:24–25:

> The God who made the world and everything in it is the Lord of heaven and earth and does not live in temples built by hands. And he is not served by human hands, as if he needed anything, *because he himself gives all men life and breath and everything else.*

Paul said to the Athenians, God gives "all men life and breath and everything else." He is constantly giving grace to people. He is constantly pouring out his goodness on the righteous and evil alike. Sometimes, people think of God as being stingy, as though we have to plead with him to give us good things. However, this is far from true. Look at how Christ described God's desire to give good things to his children:

> Which of you fathers, if your son asks for a fish, will give him a snake instead? Or if he asks for an egg, will give him a scorpion? If you then, though you are evil, know how to give good gifts to your children, how much more will your Father in heaven give the Holy Spirit to those who ask him!
> Luke 11:11–13

Christ, while instructing his disciples on how to pray (Lk 11:1), encourages them to pray by teaching them about God's desire to give good gifts. He compares God's desire to give good gifts to a parent trying to feed his son. Typically, when you see parents trying to feed, especially, little children, the parent is not reluctant. The parent is running around, trying to get the child to take one more bite. They are trying to corral the child to open his mouth to eat what is good for him. Psalm 81:10 says, "...Open wide your mouth and I will fill it." It is the child who is reluctant in receiving the food, not the parent's reluctance in giving it. Jesus says if parents, who are evil, feed their children and give them good gifts, how much more will the heavenly Father give good gifts to those who ask him? God is not only the source of good things, but he desires to give his children good things, just like a parent does.

James 1:5 says this: "If any of you lacks wisdom, he should ask God, who gives generously to all without finding fault, and it will be given to him." In describing God's desire to give wisdom to his children, especially when going through trials, he says God gives generously to those who ask him. In fact, James later says that many people have not received his gifts simply because they haven't asked (James 4:2). They are not willing to come to the source of all good things, and therefore, they receive nothing.

God is not only the standard of good things, but he is also the source of all good things, and therefore, we should seek his face for his blessing. Christ taught us in the Lord's Prayer to ask for our "daily bread" (Matt 6:11). Now, Scripture never teaches us that God wants to make us wealthy and healthy, but God is all about blessing us in order to better build his kingdom and bring glory to his name (cf. Gen 12:2-3). Those are the types of good things he wants to give. Jesus declared "Blessed are those who hunger and thirst for righteousness for they shall be filled" (Matthew 5:6). God promises to fill our desire for truly good things—for things that are righteous.

God's Goodness Should Provoke Christians to Hedonism

What should the believer's response to God's goodness be? Paul said in 1 Timothy 4:4-5, "For everything God created is good, and nothing is to be rejected if it is received with thanksgiving, because it is consecrated by the word of God and prayer."

Everything God created is good and is to be received with thanksgiving. Paul writes this in the context of teaching about false teachers who would forbid marriage and also certain foods (v. 3). Many Christians believe that if you are a Christian, you should not have any fun. Much of Christianity is full of all kinds of legalism, keeping Christians from things that God nowhere forbids in Scripture.

Let us remember that one of Satan's first temptations was to hinder the enjoyments of God's creation. He tried to implant the lie into the woman's head that "all the trees" of the garden were forbidden. In the same way, many Christians get snared by man-made laws that forbid them of the enjoyment of God's creation. Listen to what Paul told the rich people in Timothy's congregation:

> Command those who are rich in this present world not to be arrogant nor to put their hope in wealth, which is so uncertain, but to put their hope in God, *who richly provides us with everything for our enjoyment.*
> 1 Timothy 6:17

Paul told the rich people that God richly provides us with everything for our enjoyment. In a sense, Christians should have the most fun and pleasure in life. This is true because we see all these things as gifts from God. God wants us to enjoy food, he wants us to enjoy leisure, he wants us to enjoy the season of our youth, he wants us to enjoy work, etc. These are his gifts to us, created for our pleasure and enjoyment. Listen to what Solomon said, who was the wisest man on the earth:

> Then I realized that it is good and proper for a man to eat and drink, and to find satisfaction in his toilsome labor under the sun during the few days of life God has given him—for this is his lot. *Moreover, when God gives any man wealth and possessions, and enables him to enjoy them, to accept his lot and be happy in his work—this is a gift of God*. He seldom reflects on the days of his life, because God keeps him occupied with gladness of heart. Ecclesiastes 5:18–20

Solomon said he realized (meaning this was something he did not previously understand) that it was good for man to eat, drink, and find satisfaction in his labor and that this was a gift from God (v. 18). He understood that wealth and possessions were given by God to be enjoyed (v. 19). These truths do not change the fact that Christians are called to be disciplined with their earthly treasures (Matt 6:19), and that in whatever we enjoy, we must not cause offense to other brothers (Romans 14:21). But in the confines of what is moral and loving, there is freedom and encouragement to enjoy. Christians are called to be hedonists as we enjoy God's gifts and always focus on the Giver of all good gifts.

God's Goodness Should Provoke Christians to Worship

How else should God's goodness affect us?

God's goodness should always provoke worship and thanksgiving. Because we realize where every good and perfect gift comes from, it should always prompt us to give glory to God. Look at what the Psalmist said:

> Give thanks to the LORD, for he is good; his love endures forever.
> Psalm 107:1

> Let them give thanks to the LORD for his unfailing love and his wonderful deeds for men.
> Psalm 107:8

The believer should always respond with worship and thanksgiving to God since he is the giver of all good things. It should be noted, as we talk about God's goodness, that Scripture declares that God uses everything—all events—for the believer's good. Romans 8:28 says: "And we know that in all things God works for the good of those who love him, who have been called according to his purpose."

Even though God gives a common grace, a common goodness, to all, he gives a special grace only to believers. For the believer, every event is working out to his good in order to make him into the image of Christ (cf. Romans 8:29). And for this reason, a believer should give thanks in every situation (1Thessalonians 5:18).

Like Job, the believer can give thanks even in difficulties because he knows God's hand and goodness are on it. Job declared, "The Lord gives, he takes away, blessed be the name of the Lord" (Job 1:21). Believers should respond to God's goodness by worshiping and saying, "Thank you."

How often do you tell God thank you?

God's Goodness Should Provoke Christians to Good Works

How else should God's goodness make the believer respond?

Not only should God's goodness provoke us to hedonism, thanksgiving, and worship, but it should also provoke us to practice good works. Listen to Christ's reasoning behind loving and blessing our enemy:

> But I tell you: Love your enemies and pray for those who persecute you, *that you may be sons of your Father in heaven.* He causes his sun to rise on the evil and the good, and sends rain on the righteous and the unrighteous.
> Matthew 5:44–45

Christ essentially says, "Love your enemies and pray for them because your father also blesses both the good and evil. Do it because your father does it." God's goodness should draw his children to practice good works.

Galatians 6:10 says this: "Therefore, as we have opportunity, let us do good to all people, especially to those who belong to the family of believers." As the opportunities arise, let us do good to all people, but especially to those who are saved. Let us be zealous in our giving, let us be zealous in our praying, let us be zealous in acts of mercy

47

because we have a Father who is always doing good. Let us, therefore, always do good as well.

What does God's characteristic of goodness mean?

God's goodness means that he is the standard of all that is good and that everything he does is ultimately good. Understanding this reality should make us seek to enjoy God's gifts. It should constantly draw us to worship, thanksgiving, and ultimately to practice good works, as children representing their good Father.

Reflection

1. What does the goodness of God mean?
2. What should be our response to the goodness of God?
3. What other questions or thoughts do you have about this section?
4. In what ways can you pray in response? Take a second to pray as the Lord leads.

God Is Eternal

Another characteristic of God is that he is eternal. His eternality essentially means that he has no beginning and no ending. Everything else has a beginning but God does not. In fact, he is the one who created time. We see this in Genesis 1:1: "*In the beginning* God created the heavens and the earth." The question we should ask is, "In the beginning of what?" Moses, the author, is referring to time. When God created the earth, he also created time. Later in the Genesis narrative, he created the sun and moon specifically to track the time. It says, "Let there be lights in the expanse of the sky to separate the day from the night, and let them serve as signs to mark seasons and days and years" (Gen 1:14). God is eternal, and he is the beginning of all things.

In fact, we see God's eternality in the covenant name he gave to Israel. Moses said, "Who shall I tell the people sent me?" God said, tell them, "*I am* sent you" (Ex 3:13–14). "I am", or Yahweh, refers to the self-existent one, the one who always has been. I am because my parents were, but God just is; he is eternal. Jesus used this phrase to describe himself in his discussion with the Jews in John 8:57-58. It says, "'You are not yet fifty years old,' the Jews said to him, 'and you have seen Abraham!' 'I tell you the truth,' Jesus answered, 'before Abraham was born, *I am!*'". He was declaring himself to be the God of Israel (Ex 3:13–

14), but he also was declaring that he always existed, as he had previously seen Abraham.

Jesus also declared his eternality in Revelation 1:8. Listen to what he says: "I am the Alpha and the Omega," says the Lord God, "who is, and who was, and who is to come, the Almighty". Alpha and Omega are the first and last letters of the Greek alphabet. Christ was calling himself the beginning and the end. He was again declaring his eternality.

This characteristic is taught throughout the Scriptures. The Psalmist said this about God: "Before the mountains were born or you brought forth the earth and the world, *from everlasting to everlasting you are God*" (Psalm 90:2).

Reflected in the Way God Speaks about Time

Understanding God's eternality will help us better understand how he often speaks about time and events. Because he is eternal, he has a different view of time than us, and this often is reflected in his declarations.

Listen to what Peter says: "But do not forget this one thing, dear friends: With the Lord *a day is like a thousand years, and a thousand years are like a day*" (2 Peter 3:8). To God, a thousand years happens as fast as one day, but also, one day happens as slow as a thousand years. His idea of time is very different from ours since he is eternal.

Not only does he see time differently, but he is outside of time. He sees the end from the beginning. Look at Isaiah 46:10: "I make known the end from the beginning, from ancient times, what is still to come. I say: My purpose will stand, and I will do all that I please." God stands outside of time, and therefore, he sees what happened in the past, what's happening right now, and what will happen at the end. His view is very different from ours.

Reflected in the Way God Speaks about Man

We see God's unique viewpoint in how he often speaks about man. Look at what he says to Jeremiah: "Before I formed you in the womb I knew you, before you were born I set you apart; I appointed you as a prophet to the nations" (Jeremiah 1:5).

How can God know Jeremiah before he was born? Well, part of the reason is because God is outside of time. He sees Jeremiah before he was born and, at the same time, sees his end. He speaks blessing and purpose over his life before he was formed in the womb.

Look again at how he talks about all believers in Romans 8:29–30:

> *For those God foreknew he also predestined* to be conformed to the likeness of his Son, that he might be the firstborn among many brothers. And those he predestined, he also called; *those he called, he also justified; those he justified, he also glorified.*

In Romans 8:29-30, he says not only did he know and predestine believers before time (cf. Eph 1:4-5), but justified them and glorified them. Glorification specifically is an event which only happens at the rapture. It is then that we receive a glorified body. The believers in Rome that Paul was writing to had not yet died and certainly had not been glorified. However, Paul spoke about these events in the past tense. This is a reflection of God's eternality. They, as all believers, were predestined, called, justified, and glorified. These are words that only can be spoken by the

Eternal One. They reflect his unique viewpoint. He sees the end from the beginning. In God's view, believers are already saved even before they are born. They are glorified in heaven with new bodies before they even died.

Certainly, we can get a very minute understanding of God's view in comparison to ours just by looking at a child and his father. The child drops his cookie and cries because it is lost, but the father does not cry because he knows he will simply buy the child another cookie. They have different views because the father has a broader view and more life experience than the child.

In an infinitely bigger way, God sees the end from the beginning. He knows what our present trials are meant to breed and develop in our lives and what their final end will be. He can speak comfort to us because he sees the end from the beginning. He looks at our situation from an eternal viewpoint.

Reflected in Prophecy

It should be added that this eternal viewpoint is also reflected in prophecy. Often when God gives a prophecy in Scripture, it can be confusing for us. Let me give you an example. Let's look at Isaiah's prophecy of Jesus's birth:

> *For to us a child is born, to us a son is given, and the government will be on his shoulders.* And he will be called Wonderful Counselor, Mighty God, Everlasting Father, Prince of Peace.
> Isaiah 9:6

In the first part of the verse, God prophesies about the coming messiah; however, he places Christ's first coming and second coming right next to one another. It says, "For to us a child is born, to us a son is given, and the government will be on his shoulders." At Christ's first coming, he came as a child and a son, but the "government resting on his shoulders" will not be seen till his second coming, when he sets up his kingdom on the earth. This prophecy confused many of the Jews and that is why they rejected Christ. They were waiting for a conquering king, but Christ, at his first coming, came as a humble servant.

The confusion is taken away when we better understand God's eternality. God, who is outside of time, sees both of these events happening together, though there is at least two thousand years between the two comings up to this point. To God, a thousand years is like one day.

When we read the Scriptures that speak about God, we must be aware of his eternality lest we become confused. The fact that he is outside of time is seen in much of his speech and specifically his prophecies. We serve an everlasting God, an eternal God with no beginning and no end. When studying his revelation, we see this viewpoint as prevalent throughout Scripture.

Applications

How should we respond to God's eternality?

1. Understanding God's eternality teaches us to be patient.

God does not operate according to our timetable. With Abraham, he promised him a nation and a land, but Israel did not become a nation for 400 years. Even now, they are still fighting for a land. In addition, the seed he promised Abraham wasn't born until he was 100 years old.

Scripture says many of the people of God did not receive what they were waiting for. Listen to Hebrews 11:13:

> *All these people were still living by faith when they died.* They did not receive the things promised; they *only saw them and welcomed them from a distance.* And they admitted that they were aliens and strangers on earth.

God's timing is not our timing. David is still waiting for his seed to have an everlasting rule on the Davidic throne (2 Sam 7:13). Abraham is still waiting for his seed to have the land of Israel as an eternal inheritance (Gen 13:15). Understanding God's eternality should help us become more patient.

2. Understanding God's eternality should draw us to worship.

Our God is not like us. He is eternal and we are finite. This aspect of him should cause us to praise him. He is eternal.

Reflection

1. What does God's eternality mean?
2. How do we see God's eternality reflected in Scripture, and how should God's eternality affect our relationship with God?
3. What other questions or thoughts do you have about this section?
4. In what ways can you pray in response? Take a second to pray as the Lord leads.

God Is Omnipresent

Another characteristic of God is his omnipresence. This means "that God is everywhere present with His whole being at all times."[9] Listen to what David said about God:

> Where can I go from your Spirit? Where can I flee from your presence? If I go up to the heavens, you are there; if I make my bed in the depths, you are there. If I rise on the wings of the dawn, if I settle on the far side of the sea, even there your hand will guide me, your right hand will hold me fast.
> Psalm 139:7–10

David said there was nowhere he could run from God's presence, not the heavens, not hell, not the sea, and not the sky. God was everywhere. In the same way, we cannot run from God because he is always present in all places, at all times.

Applications

How should God's omnipresence affect us?

1. God's omnipresence should give us a sense of accountability.

God is not just at church on Sunday or present when we read our Bible; he is there even when we sin and are in rebellion towards his plans for our lives.

We get a picture of this with Jonah, who runs from God's calling to preach repentance to the city of Nineveh. He goes out to the sea in a boat, but there God meets him in a storm. He was tossed into the sea by the crew to preserve their lives, but there God saves him by allowing him to be swallowed by a large fish. Jonah then fulfills God's original plan for him by calling Nineveh to repentance; however, he does it with wrong motives. Later, God meets with Jonah under the shade of a vine in order to deal with the sin in his heart. There was no place to run from God, and this reality should give us a sense of accountability.

Listen to what James says, "Don't grumble against each other, brothers, or you will be judged. *The Judge is standing at the door!*" (James 5:9). James commands these Jewish Christians, scattered because of persecution (James 1:1), to live without grumbling and complaining because the Judge was standing at the door. He challenges them to live holy lives because God was always near them, ready to discipline them.

God is omnipresent, he is everywhere, but he is in different places doing different things. He is one place to empower and comfort, and in another place to judge. Understanding this reality should create a sense of accountability in us.

2. God's omnipresence should give us encouragement to serve the Lord.

We see Christ speak of his presence as an encouragement to serve and do ministry. Look at what he tells his disciples in Matthew 28:19–20:

> Therefore *go and make disciples of all nations*, baptizing them in the name of the Father and of the Son and of the Holy Spirit, and teaching them to obey everything I have commanded you. *And surely I am with you always, to the very end of the age.*

Christ gives his omnipresence as a comfort to the disciples and us, as we preach and share the gospel. If it is in front of a court or a classroom, if it's in a place where we feel scared or intimidated, we can take comfort from the fact that Christ is there with us to encourage and empower us.

It is probably this same type of encouragement we see given in the book of Philippians as the church is called to let their gentleness or care for others be known to all. Listen to what Paul says: "Let your gentleness be evident to all. *The Lord is near*" (Philippians 4:5).

Let this truth encourage us to be faithful in giving, serving, and ministering to one another because God's presence is near. He is near us to give us grace and strength. He is near to carry us and empower us to do his works. Our Lord is near.

3. God's omnipresence should give us comfort when discouraged.

The Psalmist said, "The LORD is close to the brokenhearted and saves those who are crushed in spirit" (Psalm 34:18).

The word "close" can also be translated "near" the brokenhearted. God is near us in our pain and near us in our distress in a special way. His omnipresence gives us accountability, gives us encouragement for ministry, and also comforts us in pain.

What about Hell?

What does God's omnipresence say about hell? Sometimes believers say *hell is the absence of God*. This is not true, for this would contradict the "omnipresence of God" and the "sovereignty" or "providence of God."

Colossians says he "holds all things together" (Col 1:17). Just as we cannot exist without God, neither can hell. He is even present there; he is present holding it together, but also specifically present for judgment. Consider Amos 9:1–4 and how it describes God being present to judge.

> I saw the Lord standing by the altar, and he said: "Strike the tops of the pillars so that the thresholds shake. Bring them down on the heads of all the people; those who are left I will kill with the sword. Not one will get away, none will escape. Though they dig down to the depths of the grave, from there my hand will take them. Though they climb up to the heavens, from there I will bring them down. Though they hide themselves on the top of Carmel, there I will hunt them down and seize them. Though they hide from me at the bottom of the sea, there I will command the serpent to bite them. Though they are driven into exile by their enemies, there I will command the sword to slay them. I will fix my eyes upon them for evil and not for good.

When looking at God's presence, we must realize he is present everywhere. The question is, "What is he present for?" In hell, Scripture would say he is present to bring judgment instead of blessing. With those serving God in ministry, he is present to empower. With the brokenhearted, he is present to encourage.

How does God's presence affect you? Does it comfort you, does it scare you, or are you ambivalent to his presence? How can you grow to be more aware of God's presence? David was so aware of it he said, "I can't get away from you" (Psalm 139). Thank you, Lord, that you are always present.

Reflection

1. What does God's omnipresence mean?
2. How do we see this reflected in Scripture, and how should God's omnipresence affect us?
3. What other questions or thoughts do you have about this section?
4. In what ways can you pray in response? Take a second to pray as the Lord leads.

God Is Omniscient

Another characteristic of God is his omniscience. If you break the word into two parts: "omni" means "all" and "science" means "knowledge." God has "all knowledge." A. W. Tozer's comments on God's omniscience are helpful. He wrote:

> God knows instantly and effortlessly all matter and all matters, all mind and every mind, all spirit and all spirits, all being and every being, all creaturehood and all creatures, every plurality and all pluralities, all law and every law, all relations, all causes, all thoughts, all mysteries, all enigmas, all feeling, all desires, every unuttered secret, all thrones and dominions, all personalities, all things visible and invisible in heaven and in earth, motion, space, time, life, death, good, evil, heaven, and hell.
>
> Because God knows all things perfectly, He knows no thing better than any other thing, but all things equally well. He never discovers anything, He is never surprised, never amazed. He never wonders about anything nor (except when drawing men out for their own good) does He seek information or ask questions.[10]

The Scripture teaches this in many ways. Look at what the writer of Hebrews says: "Nothing in all creation is hidden from God's sight. Everything is uncovered and laid bare before the eyes of him to whom we must give account" (Hebrews 4:13).

Our God sees everything, and similar to his omnipresence, this is also meant to give us a sense of accountability. In fact, Solomon said this: "The eyes of the LORD are everywhere, keeping watch on the wicked and the good" (Proverbs 15:3). His eyes are everywhere, watching both the good and the wicked.

Different from Human Knowledge

What makes God's knowledge different from ours is the fact that everything we know has been taught to us. We learn by reading books, listening to our teachers, and looking at the Internet, but God intrinsically knows everything. Listen to 1 John 3:20: "Whenever our hearts condemn us. For God is greater than our hearts, and *he knows everything.*"

Unlike us, he does not have to be taught because he innately knows everything. Listen to what Isaiah 40:13–14 says about him:

> Who has understood the mind of the LORD, or instructed him as his counselor? Whom did the LORD consult to enlighten him, and who taught him the right way? Who was it that taught him knowledge or showed him the path of understanding?

He essentially says, "What school did God go to?" He didn't go to school. He knows everything there is to know.

Potential Events

In fact, his knowledge is so vast that not only does he know actual events but potential events. Look at what Jesus said to the cities that would not repent at his preaching and miracles:

> Woe to you, Korazin! Woe to you, Bethsaida! If the miracles that were performed in you had been performed in Tyre and Sidon, they would have repented long ago in sackcloth and ashes.
> Matthew 11:21

Jesus said if the miracles that he performed in Korazin and Bethsaida, the cities of Israel, would have happened in Tyre and Sidon, they would still be standing today.

We should take great comfort in this. God knows what would have happened if you went to that university instead of this university, if you were raised in the U.S. instead of another country, if you married that person instead of this person. God knows all those things, and yet, chose or allowed you to be where you are (cf. Eph 1:11, Rom 8:28). This should give us great comfort, as we look over the events of our lives.

God Is All Wise

As we talk about God's omniscience, it should be noted that God is more than knowledgeable, he is all wise. This means *he always knows the best possible solution to every problem*. Look at what Paul calls God: "To the only wise

God be glory forever through Jesus Christ! Amen" (Romans 16:27).

He is the all wise God, and specifically for Christians, he uses this wisdom to guide every event in our lives for the good of bringing us into conformity with the image of his Son. Romans 8:28–29 says:

> And *we know that in all things God works for the good* of those who love him, who have been called according to his purpose. For those God foreknew *he also predestined to be conformed to the likeness of his Son,* that he might be the firstborn among many brothers.

Were there possible better paths, better decisions we could have made? Certainly, in some cases. However, God, in his wisdom and sovereignty, chose to allow the events in our lives to happen, good and bad, for the purpose of making us look more like Christ.

This may be hard to believe as we look at some of the events and failures of our lives or other believers' lives, but it is true. God is all wise, and he uses that wisdom to make us more like his Son. This should give us great comfort and help us trust God more. Proverbs 3:5 says this: "Trust in the LORD with all your heart and lean not on your own understanding."

Intimate Knowledge

Not only does God know what potentially would have happened, but Scripture teaches he has an "intimate knowledge" of each person. He even knows the number of hairs on our head. Luke 12:7 says, "Indeed, the very hairs of your head are all numbered. Don't be afraid; you are worth more than many sparrows."

Listen to what David says:

> "O LORD, you have searched me and you know me. You know when I sit and when I rise; you perceive my thoughts from afar. You discern my going out and my lying down; you are familiar with all my ways. Before a word is on my tongue you know it completely, O LORD.
> Psalm 139:1–4

He knows our thoughts, our sitting up, and our lying down. He is intimately involved in our lives because he loves us.

Applications

What does this mean for us? How can we apply the fact that God is omniscient?

1. God's omniscience means that we can be open with God in sharing our thoughts, fears, worries, and struggles.

In many of our relationships, we hide the truth. We often don't tell others how we are really feeling or share what is going on in our hearts for fear of rejection or misuse of the information. However, God already knows, and he understands our situation better than we do (Matt 6:8). Therefore, this should encourage us to share our most intimate concerns with God. Peter said, "Cast all your anxiety on him because he cares for you" (1 Peter 5:7).

God's omniscience is an encouragement for us to be transparent in our relationship with the Lord. He calls for us to cast our anxieties before him and to ask for our daily bread (cf. Matt 6:11).

2. God's omniscience should give us a sense of accountability, especially when we are tempted.

We may be able to hide our cheating, our lying, or our lustful thoughts from others, but we can't hide it from God. Not only does God know, but one day, he will even judge our "careless words" (Matthew 12:36). Listen again to what Hebrews 4:13 says: "Nothing in all creation is hidden from God's sight. Everything is uncovered and laid bare before the eyes of him to whom we must give account."

God knows, and we will give an account to him for our sins. This should motivate us to live righteously and also to continually confess our sins daily before him. He promises to forgive the sins that we sincerely confess before him (1 John 1:9).

3. God's omniscience should continually draw us into prayer, as we seek him for daily wisdom.

Scripture teaches that God loves to give his children wisdom. James 1:5 says, "If any of you lacks wisdom, he should ask God, who gives generously to all without finding fault, and it will be given to him."

Solomon asked for wisdom, and God gave liberally. Solomon became the wisest man on earth (1 Kings 3). In fact, in Proverbs, he told us to seek after wisdom more than silver and gold (Prov 8:10–11). Solomon said this because God wants to give it; he wants to guide us into the right paths for our lives (Prov 3:6).

4. God's omniscience should continually draw us to the study of Scripture, for Scripture is the revelation of God's wisdom.

David said this about the Word of God: "The statutes of the LORD are trustworthy, making wise the simple" (Psalm 19:7).

Let us come daily to the Word of God so we can become wise. God's omniscience should continually draw us to seek the wisdom of the one who is all knowing and all wise.

Reflection

1. What does God's omniscience mean?
2. How do we see God's omniscience reflected in Scripture, and how should it affect us?
3. What other questions or thoughts do you have about this section?
4. In what ways can you pray in response? Take a second to pray as the Lord leads.

God Is Omnipotent

What is another characteristic of God? Scripture would also teach that God is omnipotent, which means that God is all-powerful and able to do anything consistent with his own nature.[11] This is very important to us as Christians because when we look at how corrupt our nations are or how far away our friends or church communities are from God, we can take great comfort from this truth—God is all powerful. It simply means, "He's able" (Ephesians 3:20).[12] He is able to accomplish the impossible.

Power in Creation

Jeremiah said: "Ah, Sovereign LORD, you have made the heavens and the earth by your great power and outstretched arm. Nothing is too hard for you" (Jeremiah 32:17).

Jeremiah declared that one of the greatest examples of God's power is the creation of the heavens and earth. He said, "Sovereign Lord, you have made the heavens and the earth." However, it is not only the fact that he created the heavens and earth but, also, how he created them.

How did he create them? Scripture says that he just spoke. That is a lot of power. Some people on the earth speak and things get done. The president speaks and things start moving. But God speaks and the universe is created. That is how powerful God is. Listen to what David said as he meditated on God's power in Psalm 33:6–9:

> *By the word of the LORD were the heavens made, their starry host by the breath of his mouth.* He gathers the waters of the sea into jars; he puts the deep into storehouses. Let all the earth fear the LORD; let all the people of the world revere him. *For he spoke, and it came to be*; he commanded, and it stood firm.

Ex Nihilo

But what is also so wonderful about God's creation of the earth is the fact that he created it *ex nihilo*. *Ex nihilo* is a Latin phrase which means "out of nothing." Now, if we were going to build a house, we would need bricks. If we were going to make a beautiful painting, we would need paint and canvas. But for God, he doesn't need any of those materials; he can make things out of nothing.

Listen to what Paul said about God's creative powers: "This happened because Abraham believed in the God who brings the dead back to life and *who creates new things out of nothing*" (Romans 4:17 NLT).

The writer of Hebrews said this: "By faith we understand that the universe was formed at God's command, so that what is seen *was not made out of what was visible*" (Heb 11:3).

Our God can create out of nothing. You might say, "How is that possible? What about the law of thermodynamics? Energy is never created nor destroyed but only transferred." However, God is the one who created the laws of thermodynamics, and therefore, is not bound by it.

God is able. He is able to do more than we could ever ask or think (Eph 3:20). Christ said: "With man this is impossible, but with God all things are possible" (Matthew 19:26).

Qualified by His Character

"With God all things are possible." However, with that said, we need to qualify that statement. God's omnipotence is qualified by his character. Listen to what Paul said: "If we are faithless, he will remain faithful, *for he cannot disown himself*" (2 Timothy 2:13).

This means that if we are faithless in trusting God, he will remain faithful because he cannot deny or disown himself, meaning his own characteristics. Man is fickle; we love this person today, and we hate the same person tomorrow. But God's characteristics are always the same; he is faithful. God is righteous, and he can never stop being righteous. He cannot disown himself.

Therefore, God's omnipotence is qualified by the rest of his characteristics. There are some things God cannot do. For example, he cannot lie (Titus 1:2), he cannot be tempted with evil (James 1:13), and he cannot deny himself (2 Tim 2:13). Also, he always works to bring glory to his name. Therefore, God's use of his infinite power is qualified by his other attributes.

What other ways do we see God's power?

We see his power in nature, as God destroyed the earth by flood in Genesis 6-7. We see his power over death, as he resurrected his own Son (Rom 8:11). We see his power over the devil, as the devil must get permission from him as seen in Job 1. We see his power to save, as he redeems souls all throughout the earth. His power is so great that Scripture says he sustains the earth by his Word. He is always holding everything together. Hebrews 1:3 says: "The Son is the radiance of God's glory and the exact representation of his being, *sustaining all things by his powerful word.*"

Applications

How should we apply this reality in our lives?

1. In considering God's omnipotence, we should pray bigger and dream bigger.

It clearly should affect how we pray and how we live. Many have tiny prayers and tiny ambitions for their lives. They just want to live and make it through. Listen to what Matthew said about Jesus's hometown: "And he did not do many miracles there because of their lack of faith" (Matthew 13:58).

Many people never see or experience God's mighty power. They never see God use them or others greatly to expand his kingdom, to lead people to Christ, or to encourage others. Why? It is because of their lack of faith.

It's hard to talk to some Christians because you wonder if they are worshiping the same God. "I can't serve. I can't talk to people about my faith. I am scared. I can't do this. I can't do that." Yeah, you can't, but what about God?

I fear many Christians are like the Jews from Christ's hometown. Because they knew Jesus and had been raised with him, they lost their wonder of him, and therefore, struggled with believing in him—struggled with their faith.

Listen to 2 Corinthians 9:8, "And God is able to make all grace abound to you, so that in all things at all times, having all that you need, you will abound in every good work."

Don't you want a God that can make all grace abound to you? He can make sure you always have what you need in finances, food, and other resources. He can make sure that you always abound in every good work. That's the life we should want. We should want an all-grace abounding life.

Paul gives this specific promise as an encouragement for believers to be faithful and to trust in God's goodness as they serve him, particularly in the area of giving (2 Cor 9:7). He wants us to know, "He is able." Look at what else Paul said: "Now to him who is able to do immeasurably more than all we ask or imagine, according to his power that is at work within us" (Ephesians 3:20).

Our God can do more than we can ever ask or think. He is able. That is a God that we can and should believe in. That is the God we need, as we go through the trials and tribulations of life. That is the God we need, as we seek to see the nations know Christ. That is the God we need, as we pray for strongholds to be broken in our communities and our churches. We need to believe in a God that is able.

In fact, Scripture teaches that believing is the way to tap into this power. Jesus said this, "I tell you the truth, if you have faith as small as a mustard seed, you can say to this mountain, 'Move from here to there' and it will move. Nothing will be impossible for you" (Matthew 17:20). Paul prays this in Ephesians 1:18–20:

> I pray also that the eyes of your heart may be enlightened in order that you may know the hope to

which he has called you, *the riches of his glorious inheritance in the saints, and his incomparably great power for us who believe.* That power is like the working of his mighty strength, which he exerted in Christ when he raised him from the dead and seated him at his right hand in the heavenly realms.

We need our eyes awakened to this great power as well. This great power is available only to those who "believe". Are you believing for God to work in your family, your church, your neighborhood, and your city? Are you trusting in God? Our God is able.

How else should we apply God's omnipotence?

2. In considering God's omnipotence, we should be careful not to limit God.

Often when God calls us to do something, we try to limit him because we are focused on our inabilities. Moses, when he was called to lead Israel, began to question his abilities. He said, "I can't speak, I am slow of tongue." However, God confronted him with his omnipotence. "Who made the tongue?" (Ex 4:10-12). Whatever God calls us to do, he will empower us to do. We should not limit God.

In addition, we should never give up on the most rotten sinner or the worst looking situation because he is able. We should never limit God.

3. In considering God's omnipotence, we should always worship with thanksgiving.

His omnipotence is a wonderful characteristic, especially as you consider it in accordance with his love, grace, wisdom, and mercy. Our God is all-powerful, which is only fitting for one that is perfectly holy, wise, and gracious. We have seen a lot of power abused throughout history, but God never abuses his power. It is always used to the best and wisest end. For this reason, we should always worship and praise. Thank you, Lord!

Reflection

1. What does God's omnipotence mean?
2. How do we see God's omnipotence reflected in Scripture, and how should it affect us?
3. What other questions or thoughts do you have about this section?
4. In what ways can you pray in response? Take a second to pray as the Lord leads.

God Is Merciful

Mercy by definition means "compassion or forbearance shown especially to an offender or to one subject to one's power."[13] Grudem defines it as "God's goodness toward those in misery and distress."[14] The Bible teaches us that God is a God of mercy. David said this in 1 Chronicles 21:13: "I am in deep distress. *Let me fall into the hands of the LORD, for his mercy is very great*; but do not let me fall into the hands of men."

How is God's mercy great? What examples do we see of this in Scripture?

One of the stories in the Bible that most clearly displays God's mercy is the story of Ahab. He, along with his wife, Jezebel, ruled Israel and caused them to sin against God more than any other king previously. They killed many of the prophets and hunted others, including Elijah.

One time, Ahab messed up so badly that God told him that he was going to kill him and his whole family, and that none of them would have proper burials. This was the worst king in the history of Israel. Listen to how Ahab responded and what God did in 1 Kings 21:25-29:

> There was never a man like Ahab, who sold himself to do evil in the eyes of the LORD, urged on by Jezebel his wife. He behaved in the vilest manner by going after idols, like the Amorites the LORD

drove out before Israel.) When Ahab heard these words, he tore his clothes, put on sackcloth and fasted. He lay in sackcloth and went around meekly. Then the word of the LORD came to Elijah the Tishbite: "Have you noticed how Ahab has humbled himself before me? Because he has humbled himself, I will not bring this disaster in his day, but I will bring it on his house in the days of his son.

The worst king of Israel mourned before God, and God gave him mercy and favor because of it. Ahab, probably, will not be in heaven with us. No evidence indicates that he was a saved man, but because of his humility before God, the Lord had mercy on him. He did not give him what he deserved. This is amazing to consider.

Similarly, look at the display of God's mercy in the book of Amos:

This is what the Sovereign LORD showed me: He was preparing swarms of locusts after the king's share had been harvested and just as the second crop was coming up. When they had stripped the land clean, I cried out, "Sovereign LORD, forgive! How can Jacob survive? He is so small!" So the LORD relented. "This will not happen," the LORD said. This is what the Sovereign LORD showed me: The Sovereign LORD was calling for judgment by fire; it dried up the great deep and devoured the land. Then I cried out, "Sovereign LORD, I beg you, stop! How can Jacob survive? He is so small!" So the LORD relented. "This will not happen either," the Sovereign LORD said.
Amos 7:1–6

The prophet Amos saw judgments coming to Israel, which prompted him to pray for mercy, and God relented from each of them. Another story showing God's great mercy is the story of the apostle Paul. Look at how Paul describes it:

> Even though I was once a blasphemer and a persecutor and a violent man, I was shown mercy because I acted in ignorance and unbelief. The grace of our Lord was poured out on me abundantly, along with the faith and love that are in Christ Jesus.
> 1 Timothy 1:13–14

As Paul said, he was shown mercy. The man, who hunted and killed Christians, by God's grace and mercy, became perhaps the greatest apostle.

In all these stories, we see that the character of God is merciful. He delights in forgiving people and being merciful to those who don't deserve it.

Applications

How should God being merciful affect us?

1. God's mercy should compel believers to seek God's forgiveness for their sins.

First John 1:9 says: "If we confess our sins God is faithful and just to forgive us our sins and cleanse us from all unrighteousness."

This verse is abounding with mercy. When a believer confesses his sin, God forgives us for the specific sin and also cleanses us from *all* unrighteousness. When I confess known sin to God, he even forgives the sins I am unaware of. His mercy is abounding. He desires to give mercy to sinners.

Many saints walk around with condemnation about something they did or did not do in the past. This is because they don't truly have an understanding of God's great mercy. For that reason, they instead listen to and accept the condemnation of their flesh and the devil. Some have stopped going to church, some have stopped praying and reading their Bibles. They feel too guilty. Jesus took the penalty for our failures and our sins so that we could receive mercy. If we truly have a revelation of what Christ has done for us, we will run to the throne room of God constantly to receive grace and mercy in our time of need (Heb 4:16).

2. God's mercy should compel believers to pray for mercy over others.

If we understand God's mercy, it should cause us to seek and plead with him for mercy over others. At the cross, Jesus prayed, "Lord, forgive them for they know not what they do" (Luke 23:34). He asked for mercy towards his persecutors. The Lord's Prayer says, "forgive us *our* sins" as it ushers us to seek forgiveness for not only our sins but others (Matthew 6:12). In fact, listen to what Samuel said to Israel. "As for me, far be it from me that *I should sin* against the LORD by failing to pray for you" (1 Samuel 12: 23).

In 1 Samuel 12:19, the people asked Samuel to pray that they would not die for their sin of rejecting God and asking for a king. Samuel replied that he would not "sin" by failing to pray for them. We should see this as a duty from our Lord that we have been called to do, to pray for the sins of others, to pray for forgiveness, and to not sin by failing to do so.

This is often forgotten in our churches. If we truly understood this characteristic of God, we would plead with him for mercy on behalf of our nations, our communities, our families, friends, etc. The Lord's Prayer sets this as an abiding principle for the church: "Forgive us our sins." In fact, Scripture says that God seeks after people who will pray this way. Ezekiel 22:30 says this: "I looked for a man among them who would build up the wall and stand before me in the gap on behalf of the land so I would not have to destroy it, but I found none."

Do you ever ask for mercy over the sins of others? This is the same thing we saw the prophet Amos do for the nation of Israel (Amos 7:1-6). It is the same thing Moses did as he constantly asked God to forgive the nation of Israel for their sins (Ex 32:9-14). It is the same thing Stephen did as he asked for forgiveness over those stoning him (Acts 7:60). It is the same thing that Christ prayed for on the cross. "Lord, forgive them for they know not what they are doing" (Lk 23:34). It is the same thing we must constantly do for those around us. God has called us to be priests that make intercession for people who are far away from God (1 Peter 2:9, 1 Tim 2:1-4).

3. God's mercy should compel believers to practice mercy.

The Beatitudes give mercy as a continuing attitude and action of the redeemed. Listen to Matthew 5:7: "Blessed are the merciful, for they will be shown mercy."

In the Beatitudes, Christ is teaching the attitudes that are within those who are truly part of the kingdom of

God. With this specific attitude of mercy, Jesus gives a reciprocal promise. He says mercy will be given to those who have shown mercy. Those who practice mercy in their daily lives: forgiving others, giving to the poor, etc., will always receive mercy from God. But those who do not show mercy, God will show his justice. Matthew 6:15 says, "But if you do not forgive men their sins, your Father will not forgive your sins."

Certainly, this should be a warning to us. If we withhold mercy, God will withhold mercy from us—he will not forgive us. But even worse than withholding mercy, he will judge us for not being merciful as he is. Listen to the end of the Parable of the Unforgiving Servant:

> Shouldn't you have had mercy on your fellow servant just as I had on you?' In anger his master turned him over to the jailers to be tortured, until he should pay back all he owed. "This is how my heavenly Father will treat each of you unless you forgive your brother from your heart."
> Matthew 18:33–35

Christ declared that torment awaited those who were not merciful. This torment is probably implemented by demons as seen with Saul and those in the early church who were handed over to Satan (cf. 1 Sam 16:14, 1 Cor 5:5, 1 Tim 1:20). How many Christians are under demonic torment because of a grudge they hold against somebody that hurt them or because they have been harsh towards others instead of merciful? This is a warning Christ gave to his apostles, and, certainly, we must heed it as well.

However, Scripture promises blessing to those who are merciful. Not only will they receive mercy but also other graces from God as well. Proverbs 19:17 says, "He who is kind to the poor lends to the LORD, and he will reward him for what he has done." Proverbs 11:25 says, "A generous man will prosper; he who refreshes others will himself be refreshed." Reward and refreshment await those who relieve others of their pain through acts of mercy.

As we consider these promises, it should be a tremendous *encouragement to those serving in mercy ministries*. Mercy ministries often burn people out. However, God promises to reward and refresh us for our faithful service. Let us, especially, hold onto God's promise of refreshment. God refreshed Christ with the ministry of angels (Mark 1:13). He refreshed Elijah with food that was brought by ravens (1 Sam 17:4). David was strengthened in the Lord (1 Sam 30:6). We should hold on to God's promises.

Secondly, it also should be an *encouragement to those who are burnt out or too depressed to serve*. Sometimes, the best way to receive encouragement or relief is to have mercy on others, for then, God will have mercy on us. When discouraged, we often isolate ourselves and become consumed only with our problems. However, in ministering to others, God ministers to us. Christ promised that in taking on his yoke of service, we would find rest for our souls (Matt 11: 29). This is a challenge to the life of self-centeredness. It is a life about others that is full of refreshment and the blessings of God.

Understanding that this is a characteristic of God should cause us to practice the discipline of being merciful. By practicing mercy, we will look more like our Father who is great in mercy, and it also is the doorway to receiving tremendous blessings in our lives.

4. God's mercy should compel believers to love mercy.

Listen to what Micah 6:8 says: "He has showed you, O man, what is good. And what does the LORD require of you? To act justly and *to love mercy* and to walk humbly with your God."

Micah says we must not only show mercy but love it. It is very possible for our acts of kindness and forgiveness toward others to have the wrong motive or simply to be done out of obligation. First Peter 4:9 says, "Offer hospitality to one another without grumbling."

God not only commands our actions but he commands our hearts. He commands us to love our neighbors as ourselves and to love him with all our heart, mind, and soul. God has called for us to love showing mercy because he loves showing mercy.

This is a wonderful characteristic of God that we must strive to show every day to those God has placed around us. God's mercy must also continually drive us to the feet of God in prayer to ask for mercy on us, our communities, our nations, and all those around us. Thank you, Lord, that you are God of mercy. Thank you, Lord, that you don't keep a record of sins, for who could stand your wrath (Psalm 130:3).

Reflection

1. Define the word *mercy*.
2. In what ways do we see God's mercy reflected throughout the Scripture?
3. In what ways is God calling us to demonstrate his mercy to the church and those around us?
4. What other questions or thoughts do you have about this section?

5. In what ways can you pray in response? Take a second to pray as the Lord leads.

God Is Loving

Since love is a difficult concept to define, Grudem's comments are helpful. He says: "*God's love means that God eternally gives of himself to others*. This definition understands love as self-giving for the benefit of others. This attribute of God shows that it is part of his nature to give of himself in order to bring about blessing or good for others."[15] In fact, Scripture defines God as love, meaning he is the expression of love and all his characteristics flow out of this. Listen to what John said: "Whoever does not love does not know God, because God is love" (1 John 4:8).

This means that it is impossible to truly know what love is unless we know God, for he epitomizes love. This is part of the reason that, looking at the world today, nobody has a good definition of love. For some, love is an emotion. If you watch any romantic comedy, without a doubt, there will always come the big question, "Do you love him?"

What does that mean?

Does it mean having butterflies in one's stomach? Does it mean two people have a good time together? We can only know what love is by looking at God. Moreover, since God is love, he was living out this love even before he created the world and everything in it. In John 17:24, Jesus says this: "Father, I want those you have given me to be with me where I am, and to see my glory, the glory you have given me because you loved me before the creation of the world."

Before God created the world, he was living in a loving relationship with the Son and the Holy Spirit. In the Trinity, there has always been a perfect loving union between the members of the God-head.

We must ask the question then, "What is love?" We must know the characteristics of love in order to better understand God and to better love one another.

Scripture declares that since believers have experienced love, they naturally should demonstrate it to one another. John, who is often called the Apostle of Love and in his Gospel was identified as "the disciple whom Jesus loved" (John 13:23), said this in 1 John 4:11: "Dear friends, since God so loved us, we also ought to love one another." Similarly, Jesus said this: "By this all men will know that you are my disciples, if you love one another" (John 13:35).

Supernatural love should mark believers. The world will know us by this love. In the New Testament, God's love is the word "agape." Because this love is so otherworldly, it was rarely used in secular Greek. However, this is the type of love that the world should see in Christians. They should see a love that doesn't make sense. It is sacrificial; it is forgiving; it blesses one's enemies; it is unconditional. It is a phenomenal love by which the world should be able to identify a believer.

What does this love look like—this agape love that defines God?

As the Trinity demonstrated love toward one another throughout eternity, Christians should also demonstrate this love. Its characteristics are as follows:

Agape Love Is Practical

God's love is practical. Listen to John again: "Dear children, let us not love with words or tongue but with actions and in truth" (1 John 3:18).

Love is not just words, and it certainly is not just feelings. It is an act of the will. It is practical. Scripture does not say, "For God so loved the world that he felt all gushy inside." No, he so loved that he gave his only Son. It was practical. Look at what else the Apostle of Love says: "If anyone has material possessions and sees his brother in need but has no pity on him, how can the love of God be in him?" (1 John 3:17).

Can this be true love John questions? How can a man love someone and not meet their needs? Surely, the love of God does not live in a man such as this. The fiancée of Solomon said something similar. Consider what she said: "He has taken me to the banquet hall, and his banner over me is love" (Song of Songs 2:4).

The fiancée of Solomon declared that when they went out to eat, everybody could tell Solomon loved her. He pulled out the chair for her; he listened to her; he took care of her needs. She was the most important person in the room. His love was like a banner that everybody could see.

Sometimes, a female dates a guy who mistreats her, neglects her, and yet, still tells everybody how much they are in love. That is not love; love is practical. God's love is a giving love that provides for his people.

What else can we learn about God's love?

Agape Love Is Sacrificial

God's love is sacrificial. It cost him something. You can tell how much somebody loves you by how much they sacrifice for you. Is he or she willing to sacrifice time, money, hobbies, career, dreams, or friends for you? That is love. God so loved the world, he sacrificed himself. He sacrificed his Son. "For God so loved the world that he gave his only son" (John 3:16).

In fact, Christ demands that we love one another in the same sacrificial way. He said this: "A new command I give you: Love one another. As I have loved you, so you must love one another" (John 13:34).

How did Christ love? He died for us, and therefore, we must be willing to die for one another as well. We see something of this sacrifice in the early church. In Acts 2, the wealthy sold all they had to take care of the poor (v. 44-45). This was a sacrificial love. It was a love that distinguished them from the world. It was agape.

Are we willing to sacrifice time, job, and career in order to love God and people? True love is sacrificial.

Agape Love Is Enduring

As a Reserve military chaplain, when talking to struggling married couples, I often ask them, "What happened? How did things get so bad?" Sometimes, I get the answer, "Oh, Chaplain, nothing happened. We just fell out of love." "You fell out of love? You woke up in the morning one day and it was just gone?"

This is how most people think about love. It is something elusive. It is here one day and gone tomorrow, but that is not what Scripture teaches us about true love. Agape love is everlasting. Look at what Scripture says about God's love:

> For I am convinced that neither death nor life, neither angels nor demons, neither the present nor the future, nor any powers, neither height nor

depth, nor anything else in all creation, will be able to separate us from the love of God that is in Christ Jesus our Lord.
Romans 8:38–39

If you have been saved and have received God's love, life can't separate you from it, death can't separate you from it, and even demons can't separate you from it. The past, present, and future can't separate you from it. Nothing will be able to separate you from the love of God.

That is comforting. It tells us something about true love. It lasts. It lasts because it is an act of the will. I will marry you, and I am going to choose to love you forever, no matter what. That is God's love. It's enduring even through failures and hard times. Listen to what Paul says: "Love does not delight in evil but rejoices with the truth. It always protects, always trusts, always hopes, always perseveres" (1 Corinthians 13:6-7).

Love always perseveres. It is enduring. "And now these three remain: faith, hope and love. But the greatest of these is love" (1 Corinthians 13:13).

Agape Love Is Selfless

Listen again to what 1 Corinthians 13:5 says, "Love is *not self-seeking.*"

See, most love is selfish. It is about what we can get out of somebody. If you call me, I will call you. If you give, I will give back. Human love is very selfish. If I don't get what I want, then I don't love you anymore. If you hurt me, it's over. On the contrary, true love is all about the benefit of the other person. It is not self-seeking. Philippians 2:3-5 says this:

Do nothing out of selfish ambition or vain conceit, but in humility consider others better than yourselves. Each of you should look not only to your own interests, but also to the interests of others. Your attitude should be the same as that of Christ Jesus:

Our attitude must be the same as Christ. It must be selfless instead of selfish. This was the mindset that led Christ to die on the cross for the sins of the world. It was a mind that cared more about others and their benefit than his own. True love is selfless.

What else can we know about God's love?

Agape Love Is Unconditional

But God demonstrates his own love for us in this: While we were still sinners, Christ died for us.
Romans 5:8

God loved us while we were still sinners. He did not wait for us to clean ourselves up and to ask for forgiveness before he loved us. No, it was an unconditional and undeserved love. No strings were attached.

Our love is conditional. "I will love you if you do not cheat on me. I will love you as long as you treat me well, but when you fail me, we're done." However, we cheat on God all the time. In James 4:4, he called the church "adulterers," but that didn't stop his love for them. He would always love them unconditionally, with no strings attached. Our love must be unconditional as well.

Be imitators of God, therefore, as dearly loved children and live a life of love, just as Christ loved

us and gave himself up for us as a fragrant offering and sacrifice to God.
Ephesians 5:1

Agape Love Is Judicial

Some people have a hard time reconciling God's love and justice. But justice is an outworking of love. Listen to Hebrews 12:6: "Because the Lord disciplines those he loves, and he punishes everyone he accepts as a son."

Everybody he loves, he disciplines. For the believer, God will allow trials to happen in their lives to discipline them in order to make them more holy and righteous. Proverbs 13:24 says the same thing about parents: "He who spares the rod hates his son, but he who loves him is careful to discipline him." Agape love is judicial.

Agape Love Is Emotional

Sometimes, believers talk as though agape love is only an act of the will. It is not; affections often come along with true love. However, emotions do not define love as many in the secular world would say. Listen to Philippians 1:8: "God can testify how I long for all of you *with the affection of Christ Jesus.*"

Paul said he loved the church with the affection of Christ. "Affection" was a physical word for the stomach or bowels. He loved the church with the same feeling Christ felt in his stomach for them. True love is emotional. "Rejoice with those who rejoice; mourn with those who mourn" (Romans 12:15).

Agape Love Is Wise

93

Paul said this:

> And this is my prayer: that your love may abound more and more in knowledge and depth of insight, so that you may be able to discern what is best and may be pure and blameless until the day of Christ.
> Philippians 1:9–10

A person can love anything, even something that is bad for them. Love is so powerful it must be guided by *knowledge and depth of insight*. He essentially says, "I pray for your love to be wise so you can discern what is best."

Often "love" can lead us into things that are unhealthy for us and others, but agape love is a wise love. It is always seeking the best course of action for the other person and for ourselves.

I see that with my wife in parenting. Because my wife loves our daughter, she is very zealous in getting rid of anything that might be harmful. "Oh, that's plastic and it has chemicals; let's use something else instead." You often see this wise and discerning love with parents.

Agape love is not blind and it's not dumb. It's wise and discerning, seeking the best course of action for all.

Application

How should we apply the fact that God is loving to our lives?

1. God's love should comfort us and remove fear because God will always do what's best for us.

   Listen to Romans 8:31–32:

94

What, then, shall we say in response to this? If God is for us, who can be against us? He who did not spare his own Son, but gave him up for us all—*how will he not also, along with him, graciously give us all things?"*

God has already given his best in his Son; won't he graciously give us all things with Christ? Won't he provide whatever is beneficial since he has already given his best? If he closes the door for something, surely, it is out of love because he wants the best for us. Listen to what John said: "There is no fear in love. But perfect love drives out fear, because fear has to do with punishment. The one who fears is not made perfect in love" (1 John 4:18).

John says we should have no fear because of God's love. When love is perfected in our lives, it takes away fear. It takes fear away because we are convinced God loves us and is always working things out for our good (Rom 8:28).

2. God's love should produce the fruits of love in our lives.

Those who have truly received love should naturally demonstrate it to others. We often see this with children who are unruly. When children come from a background lacking love or filled with abuse, they often are abusive, unforgiving, and cold. But those raised in love, often are very loving.

Scripture says this should be true of every believer as well. Look at what John says:

Dear friends, let us love one another, for love comes from God. Everyone who loves has been

born of God and knows God. Whoever does not love does not know God, because God is love.
1 John 4:7–8

Everyone who loves like we have talked about is born of God and knows God. Whoever doesn't love is not from God. No matter what our background is, if we have been born again, the love of God has been shed abroad in our hearts (Rom 5:5), and it will be our tendency to love, forgive, serve, and bless others. Yes, we are not perfect yet, but we should be growing in this because we have experienced love.

Are you demonstrating love?

Reflection

1. What are characteristics of God's love?
2. What aspect of God's love was most challenging to you and why?
3. What other questions or thoughts do you have about this section?
4. In what ways can you pray in response? Take a second to pray as the Lord leads.

God Is Holy

What does God's holiness mean? John MacArthur said this:

> God is holy. Of all the attributes of God, holiness is the one that most uniquely describes Him. In reality, this is a summarization of all His other attributes. The word holiness refers to His separateness, His otherness, the fact that He is unlike any other being. It indicates His complete and infinite perfection. Holiness is the attribute of God that binds all the others together. Properly understood, it will revolutionize the quality of our worship.[16]

God's holiness is a summary of all his other characteristics. In fact, when the angels see God in heaven, they constantly declare his holiness. Isaiah 6:3 says this: "And they were calling to one another: *"Holy, holy, holy is the LORD Almighty*; the whole earth is full of his glory."

The fact that they say it three times means that it is emphatic; it is something very important that we do not want to miss. This is not only important because it is a primary characteristic of God, but it is also important because God commands us to be holy like him. Look at what he says in Leviticus 11:44: "I am the LORD your God; consecrate yourselves and be holy, because I am holy."

What exactly does it mean for God to be holy?

Holiness is a word that essentially means "set apart" and is closely connected to his righteousness. God's holiness is a picture of how righteous he is in every way.

Holiness Affects Man's Relationship with God

In fact, holiness is such a special characteristic of God that it affects our ability to be in his presence. When Adam sinned, he was kicked out of the garden, kicked out of the presence of God. Because Adam was not holy anymore, he could not dwell in God's presence.

With Israel, God set up a very elaborate system of sacrifices, washings, and cleansings in order for the people of Israel to live in the presence of God. They needed to be different from all the other nations around them because God dwelled in the midst of them. These regulations were meant to demonstrate that God was holy, set apart from everything common.

When Moses first met God on the mountain, God said to him, "Take off your shoes because you are on holy ground" (Ex 3:5). God's holiness is such a defining characteristic it must affect how we relate to him. Listen to what David said: "If I had cherished sin in my heart, the Lord would not have listened" (Psalm 66:18).

David said that a person who is living in unrepentant sin, which primarily is a matter of the heart, affects the power of their prayers. God will not listen to the prayers of a person who wants to hang on to his sin and, yet, be intimate with God at the same time.

In fact, this is what the writer of Hebrews said: "Make every effort to live in peace with all men and to be holy; *without holiness no one will see the Lord*" (Hebrews 12:14).

He says, without holiness, no one will see God. Ultimately, without a righteous life, no one can have a relationship with God.

Atonement

Well, how does this work and how can man then come into God's presence since every man has sinned (Romans 3:23)?

In the Old Testament, God set up a sacrificial system to teach man about something called *substitution*. Because God is holy and righteous, he must punish sin. Therefore, God would symbolically punish the sins of man on a sacrificed lamb so the people could enter his presence and worship him.

In fact, many scholars see "substitution" implied in the very first death. After Adam sinned, God immediately killed an animal and clothed Adam and Eve (Gen 3:20). The wages of sin is death (Romans 6:23), and therefore, someone had to die for Adam's sin. From the very beginning, God showed mercy to man by providing a substitute.

However, the sacrificial animal could never take away the sins of the world; it was only a symbol of a future reality. When John the Baptist saw Jesus, he said this: "Look, the Lamb of God, who takes away the sin of the world!" (John 1:29).

Jesus was the perfect lamb that all the sacrificial lambs always symbolized. He was man's substitute. It was only through his righteous life and death that man could be holy, and therefore, truly have a relationship with a holy God. In fact, the death of Christ was applied to all the ancient saints who died before Christ lived. Listen to what Paul said:

God presented him as a sacrifice of atonement, through faith in his blood. He did this to demonstrate his justice, because in his forbearance he had left the sins committed beforehand unpunished— he did it to demonstrate his justice at the present time, so as to be just and the one who justifies those who have faith in Jesus.
Romans 3:25–26

Revelation 13:8 says the same thing: "All inhabitants of the earth will worship the beast—all whose names have not been written in the *book of life belonging to the Lamb that was slain from the creation of the world.*"

Christ's death was applied to ancient saints from the very beginning of mankind. The sacrificial lamb was only a symbol of how God was going to save people through substitution.

Justified by Christ's Death

Because of Christ's death, God justified us, meaning he made us "just as though we never sinned." Romans 5:1 says: "Therefore, since we have been justified through faith, we have peace with God through our Lord Jesus Christ."

We can be made as though we have never sinned because of Christ's death, but it is because of his sinless life that righteousness can be applied to our account as we put our faith in him (Rom 3:26). Paul said this: "God made him who had no sin to be sin for us, so that in him we might become the righteousness of God" (2 Cor 5:21).

Not only did Jesus take the punishment for our sins, but he became sin and gave us his righteousness. In a sense, every time God sees us, he sees the righteousness of his Son. We have been made holy by the Son. This is the only way we can have a relationship with a holy God (Hebrews 12:14).

Holiness Identifies Believers

In the same way "holiness," being set apart, is a primary characteristic of God, it has now become a primary characteristic of every believer. In fact, in Scripture we are often identified by this holiness. We see this in the commonly used title "saints."

In Scripture, believers often are called "saints" which means "holy ones" because they are now set apart as positionally holy in Christ. We are holy because Christ's righteousness has been accredited to our account. Listen to how Paul commonly greeted Christians with this title:

> Paul, an apostle of Christ Jesus by the will of God, to the *saints* in Ephesus, the faithful in Christ Jesus.
> Ephesians 1:1
>
> Greet all the *saints* in Christ Jesus. The brothers who are with me send greetings. All the *saints* send you greetings, especially those who belong to Caesar's household.
> Philippians 4:21-22

Our identity is tied to Christ's righteousness and not to our failures. That is why God calls us saints, set apart ones. We must learn to identify ourselves and others in accordance with Christ's work and not ours. This would greatly change how we view ourselves and others. It also would change how we approach God. Our identification with Christ's righteousness should encourage us to approach the throne of grace with boldness to receive mercy and grace in our time of need (cf. Heb 4:16). We are set apart from the rest of the world as saints in order to know, enjoy, and represent God.

Holiness Should Be the Practice of Believers

Not only are we saints who are set apart as holy, but we must now seek practical holiness in our daily lives. It is both a matter of our position as saints and also a matter of daily practice. Listen to what Peter says: "But just as he who called you is holy, *so be holy in all you do*; for it is written: "Be holy, because I am holy" (1 Peter 1:15–16).

Because God is holy, we must always seek to be holy in all our conduct. We must be separate from the world and godly in the same way our Lord is. If a person's profession of faith does not lead to a lifestyle of practicing holiness, then this person's position might not be that of a saint before God. *Position always leads to practice.* Listen to what Christ said in Matthew 7:21: "Not everyone who says to me, 'Lord, Lord,' will enter the kingdom of heaven, but *only he who does the will of my Father* who is in heaven."

Those who have truly been saved and set apart will do "the will" of the Father. We should not think that the substitution we have encountered through God's grace is without effect. It affects how God sees us, and it radically changes the life of every true believer. Paul said this: "Therefore, if anyone is in Christ, he is a new creation; the old has gone, the new has come!" (2 Corinthians 5:17).

The believer's position in Christ changes him or her into a new creation. They now desire righteousness where they previously did not, and they start to practice a life that is pleasing to God. This does not mean they will never sin, for that will not happen until the believer has a new body, without the indwelling presence of sin. But the true believer has received a new nature that compels him to seek to live a life of holiness (cf. Rom 8:13-14, 2 Cor 5:14).

Application

How does the believer grow in holiness?

1. We must grow in holiness by studying God's Word.

How do we practice this practical righteousness? We practice it not only by knowing who God is and who we now are, but by growing in the knowledge of his Word (2 Pet 2:3). Listen to how Jesus prayed: "They are not of the world, even as I am not of it. *Sanctify them by the truth; your word is truth*" (John 17:16–17).

We are set apart to be different by the Word, that's how God sanctifies us. Why then do many Christians not live holy lives? Much of it can be attributed to not living and abiding in God's Word. This is how he trains us; this is also how he gives us strength to be righteous. Many have problems stepping away from bad relationships or the entrapment of habitual sins. This power comes through his Word. Listen to what Paul said: "All Scripture is God-breathed and is useful for teaching, rebuking, correcting and training in righteousness, so that the man of God *may be thoroughly equipped for every good work*" (2 Tim 3:16–17).

Most Christians are not equipped. To be equipped means to be ready and empowered. This happens as we get into God's Word.

2. We must grow in holiness by the practice of righteousness.

James 1:27 says:

Religion that God our Father accepts as pure and faultless is this: *to look after orphans and widows in their distress* and to keep oneself from being polluted by the world.

Religion that our Father accepts practices righteous deeds. Holiness has a positive element of righteous works such as caring for orphans and widows.

3. We must grow in holiness by keeping ourselves from sin and the world.

James 1:27 says:

Religion that God our Father accepts as pure and faultless is this: to look after orphans and widows in their distress and *to keep oneself from being polluted by the world.*

The negative element of holiness is keeping oneself from the pollution of the world. We must not be conformed to this world, but transformed by the renewing of our minds (Romans 12:2). God is holy, and therefore, we must be holy.

Reflection

1. What does God's holiness mean?

2. How do we see God's holiness demonstrated throughout Scripture?
3. How can we demonstrate God's holiness?
4. What other questions or thoughts do you have about this section?
5. In what ways can you pray in response? Take a second to pray as the Lord leads.

God Is Wrathful

Very close to God's holiness is his wrath. Because he is holy, he cannot tolerate sin. We often don't like to talk about his wrath, but the Scripture is full of the wrath of God. "In fact, the Bible has more to say about God's wrath than it does about His love."[17] What exactly is the wrath of God? Tony Evans defines the wrath of God as: "His necessary, just, and righteous retribution against sin." [18]

Examples

What examples do we see of God's wrath?

We see his wrath in cursing creation after Adam's sin in the Garden of Eden (Gen 3:17). We see his wrath in destroying the earth by water in the Genesis flood (Gen 6 and 7). We see his wrath in the destruction of Sodom and Gomorrah (Gen 19). We see his wrath throughout the OT in the discipline of Israel for not obeying him; they were persecuted by their enemies and eventually exiled from the land.

Oftentimes, people try to say his wrath is only seen in the Old Testament and not in the New, but this is not true. It is clearly seen throughout the New Testament as well. In the early church, Ananias and Sapphira were both killed for lying about the profit made from selling their land

(Acts 5:1-10). In Corinth, people were sick and dying because God judged them for dishonoring the Lord's Supper (1 Cor 11:30).

We see his wrath through church discipline as the apostles and the early church handed people over to Satan, which seemed to mean kicking them out of the church (1 Cor 5:5, 1 Tim 1:20). Scripture says that, "God is a righteous judge, a God who expresses his wrath every day" (Psalm 7:11).

How do we see God's wrath every day?

1. God's wrath is seen in handing people over to the sin they desire and allowing them to reap the consequences of it.

Sometimes, in order to teach a child, a parent will allow his son or daughter to experience the consequences of disobedience. How does God do that with the world? Consider what Romans 1:18 says: *"The wrath of God is being revealed* from heaven against all the godlessness and wickedness of men who suppress the truth by their wickedness."

It says the wrath of God is being revealed. But how is it revealed? As we read the chapter, it tells us about how God allows people to practice idolatry, sexual immorality, homosexuality, and all types of other sin. He gives a society over to their desires. Some of the worst discipline is to live in a corrupt society, with corrupt leadership, and corrupt people around us. God essentially says, "Okay, fine. Do what you want." Look at how the wrath of God is displayed in this text:

Furthermore, *since they did not think it worthwhile to retain the knowledge of God, he gave them over to a*

depraved mind, to do what ought not to be done. They have become filled with every kind of wickedness, evil, greed and depravity. They are full of envy, murder, strife, deceit and malice. They are gossips, slanderers, God-haters, insolent, arrogant and boastful; they invent ways of doing evil; they disobey their parents; they are senseless, faithless, heartless, ruthless. Although they know God's righteous decree that those who do such things deserve death, they not only continue to do these very things but also approve of those who practice them.
Romans 1:28–32

Sometimes we experience God's wrath when he gives us over to the sin we desire, and we, therefore, experience the consequences of that sin.

2. God's wrath is seen in regular discipline for sin.

We see this especially with Christians. Hebrews 12:10 says, "Our fathers disciplined us for a little while as they thought best; but God disciplines us for our good, that we may share in his holiness." God disciplines his children so that they can grow in holiness.

David said this: "It was good for me to be afflicted so that I might learn your decrees" (Psalm 119:71). It was through affliction that David learned God's Word and learned how to obey it. God often disciplines people like a parent to deter them from sin and to promote righteousness. Certainly, we see this with government, which is a reflection of God's authority. Romans 13:1–4 says this:

Everyone must submit himself to the governing authorities, for there is no authority except that which God has established. The authorities that exist have been established by God. Consequently, he who rebels against the authority is rebelling against what God has instituted, and those who do so will bring judgment on themselves. For rulers hold no terror for those who do right, but for those who do wrong. Do you want to be free from fear of the one in authority? *Then do what is right and he will commend you. For he is God's servant to do you good.* But if you do wrong, be afraid, for he does not bear the sword for nothing. *He is God's servant, an agent of wrath to bring punishment on the wrongdoer.*

Through government, God commends the righteous and punishes the wrongdoer. This is to be done in reverence of God who is the ultimate authority.

We will ultimately see God's disciplinary wrath during the tribulation period. Sometimes, it is called the "wrath of the Lamb" or the wrath of Christ (Rev 6:16).

Then the kings of the earth, the princes, the generals, the rich, the mighty, and every slave and every free man hid in caves and among the rocks of the mountains. They called to the mountains and the rocks, "Fall on us and hide us from the face of him who sits on the throne and from the *wrath of the Lamb*! For the great day of their wrath has come, and who can stand?
Revelation 6:15–17

110

Revelation 3:10 describes the tribulation further. It says, "Since you have kept my command to endure patiently, I will also keep you from the hour of trial that is going to come upon the whole world to test those who live on the earth."

The tribulation will be a time of trial the whole world will go through. God will bring his wrath on the earth in retribution for all the sins that have been committed.

3. God's wrath is seen in "eternal wrath."

John 3:36 says, "Whoever believes in the Son has eternal life, but whoever rejects the Son will not see life, *for God's wrath remains on him.*"

The wrath of God abides on the unbeliever. Mankind is under a form of wrath right now for not believing in the Son, but one day, this will become an eternal wrath. Revelation 20:15 says this: "If anyone's name was not found written in the book of life, he was *thrown into the lake of fire.*"

This judgment is eternal. It will be the final display of God's wrath, as rebellious mankind, Satan, and his angels are tormented throughout eternity (Matt 25:41). This wrath will have varying degrees of punishment based on the amount of knowledge one had and also the amount of rebellion one committed. Look at how Christ described this:

> That servant who knows his master's will and does not get ready or does not do what his master wants will be beaten with many blows. But the one who does not know and does things deserving punishment will be beaten with few blows. From everyone who has been given much, much will be

demanded; and from the one who has been entrusted with much, much more will be asked.
Luke 12:47–48

Those who know God's will and do not obey it, will have a greater judgment and those who don't know God's will and disobey, will have a less strict judgment. There will be varying degrees of punishment in hell in the same way that there will be varying degrees of reward in heaven (1 Cor 3:12-15).

This seems to be exactly what the author of Hebrews is describing in Hebrews 10, as he mentions those who had received the knowledge of the truth but rejected it. Listen to what he says:

If we deliberately keep on sinning after we have received the knowledge of the truth, no sacrifice for sins is left, but only a fearful expectation of judgment and of raging fire that will consume the enemies of God. Anyone who rejected the law of Moses died without mercy on the testimony of two or three witnesses. *How much more severely do you think a man deserves to be punished who has trampled the Son of God under foot, who has treated as an unholy thing the blood of the covenant that sanctified him, and who has insulted the Spirit of grace?* For we know him who said, "It is mine to avenge; I will repay," and again, "The Lord will judge his people." *It is a dreadful thing to fall into the hands of the living God.*
Hebrews 10:26–31

112

Those who had received the truth and then ultimately rejected it through apostasy will receive a greater punishment from God.

Applications

How should we respond to the wrath of God?

1. God's wrath should create a holy fear in us.

    Scripture says, "Our God is a consuming fire" (Heb 12:29). He is not only a God of love but of wrath, and therefore, we should fear and revere him.

    Hebrews 12:28–29 says,

    Therefore, since we are receiving a kingdom that cannot be shaken, let us be thankful, and *so worship God acceptably with reverence and awe*, for our "God is a consuming fire.

2. God's wrath should encourage us to cleanse ourselves from every form of sin.

    Second Corinthians 7:1 says,

    Since we have these promises, dear friends, let us purify ourselves from everything that contaminates body and spirit, *perfecting holiness out of reverence for God* [or fear of God].

    We must pursue holiness because we fear God. Those who do not fear God, will not.

3. God's wrath should be modeled.

An aspect of God's wrath should be modeled by believers. Not all anger is sinful. Sometimes, it is sinful for us to not be angry about things that are happening in the world. To not be angry would be to fall short of the glory of God (Romans 3:23). In Mark 11, Christ went into the temple, used a whip and flipped tables because the leaders were cheating people and dishonoring God. He said, "Is it not written: 'My house will be called a house of prayer for all nations'? But you have made it 'a den of robbers'" (Mark 11:17).

A righteous anger must be developed in the life of those who follow Christ and who are seeking to imitate him (Eph 5:1).

How do we discern if we have a righteous anger or a selfish anger (James 1:19-20)?

Certainly, we can learn to distinguish by a careful study of Christ. When people were being cheated and God was being dishonored, he was like a lion. He pulled out the whip and was aggressive with a righteous anger. But when he was dishonored, he was like a lamb to the slaughter. Let's look at 1 Peter 2:21–23:

> To this you were called, *because Christ suffered for you, leaving you an example, that you should follow in his steps*. "He committed no sin, and no deceit was found in his mouth." When they hurled their insults at him, *he did not retaliate; when he suffered, he made no threats. Instead, he entrusted himself to him who judges justly.*

When Christ was treated unjustly, he turned the other cheek, and was silent. But when others were

114

mistreated, he demonstrated righteous anger. Certainly, there is a place for defending our rights and going to the authorities. Paul himself appealed to Caesar when he was being mistreated in prison (Acts 25:11). We have that right as well, but there is also a time to be silent and submit to harsh treatment (1 Cor 6:7). We must through prayer and wise counsel discern those times.

However, we also must discern when to be righteously angry. Anger is a characteristic of God that has been given to us in order for us to seek justice in the same way he does. It is needed to fight against religious corruption, unethical law practices, trafficking, abortion, racism, etc., and it is even needed for us to faithfully pray against these things. We must develop a holy anger for it is a characteristic of God.

Reflection

1. What does God's wrath mean?
2. In what events in Scripture do we see God's wrath?
3. In what ways should Christians demonstrate God's wrath?
4. What other questions or thoughts do you have about this section?
5. In what ways can you pray in response? Take a second to pray as the Lord leads.

God Is Sovereign

Is God in control of all things and if so to what extent? This is one of the most controversial aspects of the characteristics of God. Christians are divided on this issue. Some declare if God is totally in control of everything, humans are just robots with no free will.

What exactly does the Scripture say about God being in control of everything, and how does this correspond with free will and the presence of evil and Satan in the world?

Scriptures Teaches God's Sovereignty

God is in control of all things. Listen to what Ephesians 1:11 says: "In him we were also chosen, having been predestined according to the plan of him *who works out everything in conformity with the purpose of his will.*"

It does not say that God works some things according to the purpose of his will, but *all things.* Everything somehow is moving in line with God's plan, including my writing this, and your reading and thinking about it. Everything is working in conformity with the plan of God. This is a mystery, but it is clearly taught in Scripture.

How do we see this sovereignty expressed and explained in Scripture?

Romans 8:28 tells us something about his purposes in controlling all events. It says, "And we know that *in all things God works for the good of those who love him*, who have been called according to his purpose". God controls events in such a way that they always work to the good of his children.

For this reason, the doctrine of the sovereignty of God gives Christians great confidence since nothing happens outside of his control. We know that Satan isn't in control, the government isn't in control, terrorists aren't in control— God is. He is even in *control of trials*. Scripture says he holds the temperature gauge on our trials so that we are never tempted above what we are able. Look at 1 Corinthians 10:13:

> No temptation has seized you except what is common to man. And God is faithful; *he will not let you be tempted beyond what you can bear*. But when you are tempted, he will also provide a way out so that you can stand up under it.

How else do we see God's sovereignty throughout Scripture?

We see God in *control of each man's time on the earth*. Listen to what David said, "Your eyes saw my unformed body. All the days ordained for me were written in your book before one of them came to be" (Psalm 139:16).

What about a chance death or a sickness that takes somebody away? David said these were "ordained." The word "ordained" eliminates the possibility of chance. It means God is in control of our days on the earth and that they were written out beforehand.

We see God clearly described as *in control of nature*. What did Christ teach in Matthew 6 about nature?

Jesus said that God clothes the lilies of the field and he feeds the birds of the air.

> Look at the birds of the air; they do not sow or reap or store away in barns, and yet your heavenly Father feeds them. Are you not much more valuable than they? Who of you by worrying can add a single hour to his life? "And why do you worry about clothes? See how the lilies of the field grow. They do not labor or spin.
> Matthew 6:26–28

This might seem strange to us for we know all these things happen naturally. Natural processes happening in the world allow these things to happen. However, Scripture would say these things are not happening apart from God's sovereignty; he is actually working in his creation and never losing control.

We also see this in what Paul taught about Christ in Colossians 1:17: "He is before all things, *and in him all things hold together.*"

Is God a clockmaker that winds up creation and allows it to continually work on its own? Or is he somehow vitally involved and always in control of it? Paul says Christ is always holding everything together, and, in Acts, he even declares that each breath of man comes from God. "And he is not served by human hands, as if he needed anything, because *he himself gives all men life and breath and everything else*" (Acts 17:25).

What else does Scripture say God controls?

Scripture declares that God is in *control of random events* such as casting lots which is like the rolling of dice. "The lot is cast into the lap, but its every decision is from the LORD" (Prov 16:33).

It even declares that *God is in control of kings* and that he turns their hearts in whatever direction he wills. "The king's heart is in the hand of the LORD; he directs it like a watercourse wherever he pleases" (Prov 21:1).

God is in control of *disasters*. Look at what Amos says: "When a trumpet sounds in a city, do not the people tremble? *When disaster comes to a city, has not the LORD caused it?*" (3:6). Sometimes the disasters are directly a judgment for sin as seen in the Genesis flood and sometimes not as with Job and Joseph. Either way, Scripture would say that God is in control of these events.

God is in control of trials, each person's time on the earth, nature, random events, the heart of kings, and even disasters.

God's Control over Men and Evil

What about the decisions of men and evil?

Yes, Scripture also teaches that God is in control of the decisions of men and evil. In fact, it would seem to indicate that God is the first cause of these things even though he cannot be blamed because of the secondary causes. Theologians have called this the *law of concurrence*.[19] It is possible for something to have many causes. The bird has food because he went and caught the food, but God ultimately provided it for him. Satan tempted man, but God was in control as seen in the story of Job. There are many causes. Wayne Grudem's comments are helpful:

> In this way it is possible to affirm that in one sense events are fully (100 percent) caused by God and fully (100 percent) caused by the creature as well. However, divine and creaturely causes

work in different ways. The divine cause of each event works as an invisible, behind-the-scenes, directing cause and *therefore could be called the "primary cause" that plans and initiates everything that happens* (emphasis mine).[20]

In one sense, Scripture shows God as being the first cause of events simply because nothing can happen apart from his sovereign purpose and his sustaining power (cf. Eph 1:11, Heb 1:3). God sustains "all things by his powerful word" (Heb 1:3). However, again, Scripture would teach this without placing the blame on God for sin or evil (James 1:13). The sovereignty of God and, yet, human responsibility is a mystery, but Scripture teaches them both. It is a paradox—two seemingly contradicting realities.

Pharaoh's Hardened Heart

Let's consider a familiar passage with Pharaoh, the king of Egypt. Moses asks Pharaoh to let the people of Israel go even though God had already predicted that he would harden Pharaoh's heart (Ex 4:21). Then later, the narrator gives two seemingly conflicting statements. It says that Pharaoh hardened his own heart in Exodus 8:15. "But when Pharaoh saw that there was relief, *he hardened his heart* and would not listen to Moses and Aaron, just as the LORD had said." And later, it says that God hardened his heart in Exodus 14:8. "*The LORD hardened the heart of Pharaoh king of Egypt, so that he pursued the Israelites, who were marching out boldly.*"

Which is the first cause, God or Pharaoh? It teaches that both were responsible in some way or another. But since God is the sovereign, he is ultimately in control, and therefore, the first cause (cf. Prov 21:1).

Why does God harden his heart? This is what Paul says about the event in Romans 9:17–18:

> For the Scripture says to Pharaoh: "I raised you up for this very purpose, that I might display my power in you and that my name might be proclaimed in all the earth." Therefore God has mercy on whom he wants to have mercy, and he hardens whom he wants to harden.

Paul quotes a verse in Exodus saying God hardened Pharaoh's heart for his purposes, which was that his name might be proclaimed throughout all the earth. God was the first cause. In fact, we see that when Israel later entered Jericho, the people there were afraid. They had heard about God parting the Red Sea and his destruction of the Egyptians (Josh 2:10). Pharaoh's sin was used to bring glory to God.

This might give us an answer to the question, "If God is in control, why did he allow sin in the first place?" In some way or another, God's characteristics and his glory are more powerfully displayed with the reality of sin. Like a diamond against a black cloth—God's beauty is more clearly displayed against the darkness. If there was no sin, then we would never fully know the concept of God's holiness and his anger against sin. We would never fully know his characteristics of patience, grace, or mercy.

Now, the reality of God's sovereignty, as seen in his hardening Pharaoh's heart, might naturally provoke men to anger or resentment. Paul, in fact, expected that some reading his teachings about Pharaoh and God's sovereignty might respond that way. They would say, "How can God hold us accountable or blame us if he is in control of everything?" Look at his reply:

122

One of you will say to me: "Then why does God still blame us? For who resists his will?" But who are you, O man, to talk back to God? "Shall what is formed say to him who formed it, 'Why did you make me like this?' Does not the potter have the right to make out of the same lump of clay some pottery for noble purposes and some for common use?"
Romans 9:19–21

Paul simply replies to their confusion with the doctrine of God's sovereignty. The Lord is God, he is the Creator, and he does what he wants. Who are you to say to the Creator, why did you make me like this?

God's Kingship

Listen to what David says in Psalm 47:2: "How awesome is the LORD Most High, *the great King over all the earth!*"
See, this concept of God being king over the whole earth is very hard, especially for westerners, to accept because we have never had a king. But a true monarchy is not a democracy, where people get to choose. In a true monarchy, the king is in total control and does what he wishes. This is what Psalm 115:3 says: "Our God is in heaven; *he does whatever pleases him.*"
Now with that said, we can take comfort in all the other characteristics of God. He is all wise; he is good; he is righteous. He works all things out for the good. There is no better person to be in total control. That should comfort us.
With that said, God's sovereignty somehow works together with man's free will, as we saw in the case of Pharaoh. God hardened Pharaoh's heart, and yet, Pharaoh

hardened his own heart. Scripture says that even though God was in control and the first cause, Pharaoh was responsible—he made a choice.

We make choices every day, and if we sin, we are to blame. But somehow with that reality, Scripture would say God was in control. The mystery is in how these two truths can coexist. It doesn't make sense to us; however, we can be sure they make perfect sense to God.

This again reflects the *law of concurrence*; there are at least two causes. God acted and man acted. Which is the primary cause? Scripture would say God is, and therefore, there is a sense in which his will is always done (Eph 1:11).

God's Sovereignty and Satan

Now, here is the next question, we have looked at God's sovereignty in considering man's free will and specifically sin, but what about God's sovereignty over Satan? The Bible also teaches that God is in control of Satan. Let's look at a story with David in 2 Samuel 24:1: "Again the *anger of the LORD burned against Israel, and he incited David against them*, saying, 'Go and take a census of Israel and Judah.'"

This is the narrative of David counting all the soldiers in Israel and God punishing Israel because of David's pride. In the 2 Samuel narrative, it says God "incited David against them." However, when you look at the parallel passage in Chronicles, it gives a different cause behind David's census. It says in 1 Chronicles 21:1: "*Satan rose up against Israel and incited David* to take a census of Israel."

It says Satan incited David. Which one did it, God or Satan? They both did, but again, Scripture would say

God is sovereign; he is the ruler who is always working out his plans on the earth. Therefore, he is the first cause. Satan is the second cause. Scripture would teach that God is the cause because nothing can happen apart from his sovereignty. However, the paradox is that Scripture would also teach that God cannot be blamed and that he tempts no man (James 1:13). It would attribute blame both to Satan and David for they both chose to sin. This is a mystery. In some way, God's sovereignty over all things does not relinquish the blame of demons or mankind.

We see a similar case in the story of Job. In chapter 1, Satan asked God for permission to touch Job, but when Job had lost everything, Job declared God was the cause of his loss. Look at what he says:

> Naked I came from my mother's womb, and naked I will depart. *The LORD gave and the LORD has taken away*; may the name of the LORD be praised." In all this, Job did not sin by charging God with wrongdoing.
> Job 1:21–22

Job sees God in control of his loss and worships him. The author quickly adds, "Job did not sin by charging God with wrongdoing."

In addition, we see another story that teaches this truth in Micaiah's vision that was shared with both King Ahab and King Jehoshaphat. Listen to the prophecy:

> Micaiah continued, "Therefore hear the word of the LORD: I saw the LORD sitting on his throne with all the host of heaven standing around him on his right and on his left. *And the LORD said, 'Who will entice Ahab into attacking Ramoth Gilead and going to his*

death there?' "One suggested this, and another that. *Finally, a spirit came forward, stood before the LORD and said, 'I will entice him.'* "'By what means?' the LORD asked. "'I will go out and be a lying spirit in the mouths of all his prophets,' he said. *"'You will succeed in enticing him,'* said the LORD. 'Go and do it.' *"So now the LORD has put a lying spirit in the mouths of all these prophets of yours. The LORD has decreed disaster for you."*
1 Kings 22:19-23

In this prophecy, God is pictured as looking for someone to entice King Ahab so he can be led to his destruction for all the evil that he had previously committed. Apparently, a demon approaches the Lord and says that he will entice Ahab by being a lying spirit in the mouth of his prophets. God tells him to "Go and do it" and that he would be successful. Who enticed Ahab? The demonic spirit did. Who was in control? God was.

Scripture clearly declares that God is in control of all things (Eph 1:11), and yet, there can be other causes such as Satan or man. Wayne Grudem gives a very insightful conclusion to our look at how Scripture teaches God's control over both man's sin and the devil. Listen to what he says:

We must remember that in all these passages it is very clear that Scripture nowhere shows God as directly doing anything evil but rather as bringing about evil deeds through the willing actions of moral creatures. Moreover, Scripture never blames God for evil or shows God as taking pleasure in evil and Scripture never excuses human beings for the wrong they do.

However we understand God's relationship to evil, we must never come to the point where we think that we are not responsible for the evil that we do, or that God takes pleasure in evil or is to be blamed for it. Such a conclusion is clearly contrary to Scripture.[21]

With this said, there are different views on this subject. The one detailed here is primarily the Calvinistic view that is believed in many denominations, but primarily in the reformed camp such as Presbyterians and Reformed Baptists. Calvinists are in every denomination; however, Arminianism is stronger in Methodist denominations and some Pentecostals.

Wayne Grudem states the Arminian position this way:

Those who hold an Arminian position maintain that in order to preserve the *real human freedom* and *real human choices* that are necessary for genuine human personhood, God cannot cause or plan our voluntary choices. Therefore they conclude that God's providential involvement in or control of history must *not* include *every specific detail* of every event that happens, but that God instead simply *responds* to human choices and actions as they come about and does so in such a way that his purposes are ultimately accomplished in the world.[22]

However, it's difficult to come to that doctrinal conclusion because so many Scriptures address God's sovereignty and speak of "all" circumstances, not just some, in his control. One Scripture says, "In him we were also chosen, having been predestined *according to the plan of him who works out everything in conformity with the purpose of his will"* (Ephesians 1:11).

Everything is working in conformity to his "plan." They are not just happening and then he fixes them.

"And we know that in *all things* God works for the good of those who love him, who have been called according to his purpose" (Romans 8:28).

David said, "Your eyes saw my unformed body. *All the days ordained for me were written in your book before one of them came to be*" (Psalm 139:16).

The author of Hebrews said, "The Son is the radiance of God's glory and the exact representation of his being, *sustaining all things by his powerful word.* After he had provided purification for sins, he sat down at the right hand of the Majesty in heaven" (Hebrews 1:3).

"I form the light and create darkness, *I bring prosperity and create disaster*; I, the LORD, *do all these things* (emphasis mine)" (Isaiah 45:7).

"Is it not from the mouth of the Most High that both calamities and good things come?" (Lamentations 3:38).

Mundane events like eating and drinking are under his control; random events, our future, and both disaster and good things come from him. His sovereignty is absolute, total, and comprehensive. If God ceased to be in control, he would cease to be God. His sovereignty is just as much a characteristic of him as his omniscience or omnipresence.

With all that said, we must always realize an aspect of mystery comes with this doctrine. If we try to explain it without recognizing the paradox—the apparent contradiction—then we are oversimplifying God for our own understanding. Some aspects of God we cannot fully comprehend. God is the first cause of all things but only in

128

such a way that he cannot be blamed for evil. How this works, we cannot be fully sure, but we must teach it and uphold God's right as the potter to do whatever he wants since he is king (cf. Rom 9:19-21, Psalm 47:2).

Application

What are some encouragements from the fact that God is sovereign?

1. We can have comfort in the fact that there are no accidents.

Nothing happens outside of his will. Even our mistakes and the greatest evils somehow fit into God's sovereign plan (Eph 1:11).

2. We can have comfort in the fact that God can hear and respond to our prayers.

Why pray if God is not sovereign and in control of all things? It is his sovereignty that gives us confidence that he can change things or make things better. We get to talk to the God who is controlling everything and ask for his perfect will to be done on the earth. Though he is sovereign, he has chosen to work through the prayers of his people. Ezekiel 22:30 says, "I looked for a man among them who would build up the wall and stand before me in the gap on behalf of the land so I would not have to destroy it, but I found none."

3. We can have comfort in failure and difficult circumstances.

We can be comforted no matter how bad a situation is, or how badly we have failed, or what Satan has done. God is ultimately in control. We can see Joseph's comfort and also how he comforted his brothers in referring to their sin of selling him into slavery in Genesis 50:20. When his brothers asked for forgiveness, he responded with, "You intended to harm me, but God intended it for good to accomplish what is now being done, the saving of many lives." He saw God in control, and therefore, he took comfort and held no grudges. He also was calling for his brothers to take comfort in God's sovereignty, as he used even their bad intentions for good.

A person who doesn't understand and trust God's sovereignty will be a person who holds tremendous grudges and may find themselves very fearful or anxious at times. They also may find it impossible to accept God's forgiveness for their failures. God's sovereignty gives us confidence and brings comfort to our lives.

Reflection

1. In what ways do we see God's sovereignty taught in the Scriptures?
2. Why is God's sovereignty such a controversial doctrine?
3. What is the main difference between a Reformed understanding of God's sovereignty and an Arminian one? Which one do you lean toward?
4. What other questions or thoughts do you have about this section?
5. In what ways can you pray in response? Take a second to pray as the Lord leads.

Conclusion

Why is knowing the perfections of God important? It is important so we can worship him and serve him properly. The more you know him, the more your worship will be enhanced and the better you can please him (John 4:23).

What characteristics of God have we studied in the last few chapters?

1. God is spirit.
2. God is a person.
3. God is independent.
4. God is immutable.
5. God is good.
6. God is eternal.
7. God is omnipresent.
8. God is omniscient.
9. God is omnipotent.
10. God is merciful.
11. God is loving.
12. God is holy.
13. God is wrathful.
14. God is sovereign.

Walking the Romans Road

How can a person be saved? From what is he saved? How can someone have eternal life? Scripture teaches that after death each person will spend eternity either in heaven or hell. How can a person go to heaven?

Paul said this to Timothy:

> But as for you, continue in what you have learned and have become convinced of, because you know those from whom you learned it, and how from infancy you have known the holy Scriptures, which are *able to make you wise for salvation through faith in Christ Jesus.*
> 2 Timothy 3:14-15

One of the reasons God gave us Scripture is to make us wise for salvation. This means that without it nobody can know how to be saved.

Well then, how can a people be saved and what are they being saved from? A common method of sharing the good news of salvation is through the Romans Road. One of the great themes, not only of the Bible, but specifically of the book of Romans is salvation. In Romans, the author, Paul, clearly details the steps we must take in order to be saved.

How can we be saved? What steps must we take?

Step One: We Must Accept that We Are Sinners

Romans 3:23 says, "For all have sinned and fall short of the glory of God." What does it mean to sin? The word sin means "to miss the mark." The mark we missed is looking like God. When God created mankind in the Genesis narrative, he created man in the "image of God" (1:27). The "image of God" means many things, but probably, most importantly it means we were made to be holy just as he is holy. Man was made moral. We were meant to reflect God's holiness in every way: the way we think, the way we talk, and the way we act. And any time we miss the mark in these areas, we commit sin.

Furthermore, we do not only sin when we commit a sinful act such as: lying, stealing, or cheating; again, we sin anytime we have a wrong heart motive. The greatest commandments in Scripture are to "Love God with all our heart, mind, and soul and to love others as ourselves" (Matt 22:36-40, paraphrase). Whenever we don't love God supremely and love others as ourselves, we sin and fall short of the glory of God. For this reason, man is always in a state of sinning. Sadly, even if our actions are good, our heart is bad. I have never loved God with my whole heart, mind, and soul and neither has anybody else. Therefore, we have all sinned and fall short of the glory of God (Rom 3:23). We have all missed the mark of God's holiness and we must accept this.

What's the next step?

Step Two: We Must Understand We Are under the Judgment of God

134

Why are we under the judgment of God? It is because of our sins. Scripture teaches God is not only a loving God, but he is a just God. And his justice requires judgment for each of our sins. Romans 6:23 says, "For the wages of sin is death."

A wage is something we earn. Every time we sin, we earn the wage of death. What is death? Death really means separation. In physical death, the body is separated from the spirit, but in spiritual death, man is separated from God. Man currently lives in a state of spiritual death (cf. Eph 2:1-3). We do not love God, obey him, or know him as we should. Therefore, man is in a state of death.

Moreover, one day at our physical death, if we have not been saved, we will spend eternity separated from God in a very real hell. In hell, we will pay the wage for each of our sins. Therefore, in hell people will experience various degrees of punishment (cf. Lk 12:47-48). This places man in a very dangerous predicament—unholy and therefore under the judgment of God.

How should we respond to this? This leads us to our third step.

Step Three: We Must Recognize God Has Invited All to Accept His Free Gift of Salvation

Romans 6:23 does not stop at the wages of sin being death. It says, "For the wages of sin is death, but the gift of God is eternal life through Jesus Christ our Lord." Because God loved everybody on the earth, he offered the free gift of eternal life, which anyone can receive through Jesus Christ.

Because it is a gift, it cannot be earned. We cannot work for it. Ephesians 2:8-9 says, "For it is by grace you have been saved, through faith—and this not from yourselves, it is the gift of God—not by works, so that no one can boast."

Going to church, being baptized, giving to the poor, or doing any other righteous work does not save. Salvation is a gift that must be received from God. It is a gift that has been prepared by his effort alone.

How do we receive this free gift?

Step Four: We Must Believe Jesus Christ Died for Our Sins and Rose from the Dead

If we are going to receive this free gift, we must believe in God's Son, Jesus Christ. Because God loved us, cared for us, and didn't want us to be separated from him eternally, he sent his Son to die for our sins. Romans 5:8 says, "But God demonstrates his own love for us in this: While we were still sinners, Christ died for us." Similarly, John 3:16 says, "For God so loved the world that he gave his only begotten son that whosoever believeth in him should not perish but have eternal life." God so loved us that he gave his only Son for our sins.

Jesus Christ was a real, historical person who lived 2,000 years ago. He was born of a virgin. He lived a perfect life. He was put to death by the Romans and the Jews. And he rose again on the third day. In his death, he took our sins and God's wrath for them and gave us his perfect righteousness so we could be accepted by God. Second Corinthians 5:21 says, "God made him who had no sin to be sin for us, so that in him we might become the righteousness of God." God did all this so we could be saved from his wrath.

Christ's death satisfied the just anger of God over our sins. When God saw Jesus on the cross, he saw us and our sins and therefore judged Jesus. And now, when God sees those who are saved, he sees his righteous Son and accepts us. In salvation, we have become the righteousness of God.

If we are going to be saved, if we are going to receive this free gift of salvation, we must believe in Christ's death, burial, and resurrection for our sins (cf. 1 Cor 15:3-5, Rom 10:9-10). Do you believe?

Step Five: We Must Confess Christ as Lord of Our Lives

Romans 10:9-10 says,

> That if you confess with your mouth, "Jesus is Lord," and believe in your heart that God raised him from the dead, you will be saved. For it is with your heart that you believe and are justified, and it is with your mouth that you confess and are saved.

Not only must we believe, but we must confess Christ as Lord of our lives. It is one thing to believe in Christ but another thing to follow Christ. Simple belief does not save. Christ must be our Lord. James said this: "Even the demons believe and shudder" (James 2:19) but the demons are not saved—Christ is not their Lord.

Another aspect of making Christ Lord is *repentance*. Repentance really means a change of mind that leads to a change of direction. Before we met Christ, we were living our own life and following our own sinful desires. But when we get saved, our mind and direction change. We start to follow Christ as Lord.

How do we make this commitment to the lordship of Christ so we can be saved? Paul said we must confess with our mouth "Jesus is Lord" as we believe in him.

Romans 10:13 says, "Everyone who calls on the name of the Lord will be saved."

If you admit that you are a sinner and understand you are under God's wrath because of them; if you believe Jesus Christ is the Son of God, that he died on the cross for your sins, and rose from the dead for your salvation; if you are ready to turn from your sin and cling to Christ as Lord, you can be saved.

If this is your heart, then you can pray this prayer and commit to following Christ as your Lord.

> *Dear heavenly Father, I confess I am a sinner and have fallen short of your glory, what you made me for. I believe Jesus Christ died on the cross to pay the penalty for my sins and rose from the dead so I can have eternal life. I am turning away from my sin and accepting you as my Lord and Savior. Come into my life and change me. Thank you for your gift of salvation.*

Scripture teaches that if you truly accepted Christ as your Lord, then you are a new creation. Second Corinthians 5:17 says, "Therefore, if anyone is in Christ, he is a new creation; the old has gone, the new has come!" God has forgiven your sins (1 John 1:9), he has given you his Holy Spirit (Rom 8:15), and he is going to disciple you and make you into the image of his Son (cf. Rom 8:29). He will never leave you nor forsake you (Heb 13:5), and he will complete the work he has begun in your life (Phil 1:6). In heaven, angels and saints are rejoicing because of your commitment to Christ (Lk 15:7).

Praise God for his great salvation! May God keep you in his hand, empower you through the Holy Spirit, train you through mature believers, and use you to build his kingdom! "The one who calls you is faithful, he will do it" (1 Thess 5:24). God bless you!

Coming Soon

Praise the Lord for your interest in studying and teaching God's Word. If God has blessed you through the BTG series, please partner with us in petitioning God to greatly use this series to encourage and build his Church. Also, please consider leaving an Amazon review and signing up for free book promotions. By doing this, you help spread the "Word." Thanks for your partnership in the gospel from the first day until now (Phil 1:4-5).

Available:
First Peter
Theology Proper
Building Foundations for a Godly Marriage
Colossians
God's Battle Plan for Purity
Nehemiah
Philippians
The Perfections of God
The Armor of God

Coming Soon:
Abraham
Ephesians

About the Author

Greg Brown earned his MA in religion and MA in teaching from Trinity International University, a MRE from Liberty University, and a PhD in theology from Louisiana Baptist University. He has served over ten years in pastoral ministry and currently serves as Chaplain and Assistant Professor at Handong Global University, pastor at Handong International Congregation, and as a Navy Reserve chaplain.

Greg married his lovely wife Tara Jayne in 2006, and they have one daughter, Saiyah Grace. He enjoys going on dates with his wife, playing with his daughter, reading, writing, studying in coffee shops, working out, and following the NBA and UFC. His pursuit in life, simply stated, is "to know God and to be found faithful by Him."

To connect with Greg, please follow at http://www.pgregbrown.com.

144

Notes

[1] Millard J. Erickson. *Christian Theology* (2nd ed.). (Grand Rapids, MI: Baker Book House, 1998), 291.

[2] Charles C. Ryrie. *Basic Theology: A Popular Systematic Guide to Understanding Biblical Truth* (Chicago, IL: Moody Press, 1999), 39.

[3] Wayne A. Grudem. *Systematic Theology: An Introduction to Biblical Doctrine* (Leicester, England; Grand Rapids, MI: Inter-Varsity Press; Zondervan Pub. House, 2004), 167.

[4] Evans, Tony. *Theology You Can Count On.* (Chicago, IL: Moody Publishers, 2008), Kindle edition.

[5] Chariots of Fire (1981 feature film)

[6] Evans, Tony. *Theology You Can Count On* (Chicago, IL: Moody Publishers, 2008), Kindle edition.

[7] Evans, Tony. *Theology You Can Count On.* ((Chicago, IL, Moody Publishers, 2008), Kindle edition.

[8] Wayne A. Grudem, *Systematic Theology: An Introduction to Biblical Doctrine* . (Leicester, England; Grand Rapids, Mchigan: Inter-Varsity Press; Zondervan Pub. House, 2004), 197.

[9] Charles C. Ryrie. *Basic Theology: A Popular Systematic Guide to Understanding Biblical Truth* (Chicago, IL: Moody Press, 1999), 46.

[10] Charles C. Ryrie. *Basic Theology: A Popular Systematic Guide to Understanding Biblical Truth* (Chicago, IL: Moody Press, 1999), 47.

[11] Charles C. Ryrie. *Basic Theology: A Popular Systematic Guide to Understanding Biblical Truth.* (Chicago, IL: Moody Press, 1999), 45.

[12] Tony Evans. *Theology You Can Count On.* (Chicago, Illinois: Moody Publishers, 2008), Kindle edition.

[13] http://www.merriam-webster.com/dictionary/mercy (accessed on March 12, 2014).

[14] Wayne A. Grudem. *Systematic Theology: An Introduction to Biblical Doctrine.* (Leicester, England; Grand Rapids, MI: Inter-Varsity Press; Zondervan Pub. House, 2004), 200.

[15] Wayne A. Grudem. *Systematic Theology: An Introduction to Biblical Doctrine* (Leicester, England; Grand Rapids, MI: Inter-Varsity Press; Zondervan Pub. House, 2004), 198.

[16] John F. MacArthur. *Worship: The Ultimate Priority.* (Chicago, IL: Moody Publishers, 2012), Kindle edition.

[17] Evans, Tony. *Theology You Can Count On* (Chicago, IL: Moody Publishers, 2008), Kindle edition

[18] Evans, Tony. *Theology You Can Count On* (Chicago, IL: Moody Publishers, 2008), Kindle edition.

[19] Wayne A. Grudem, *Systematic Theology: An Introduction to Biblical Doctrine* (Leicester, England; Grand Rapids, Michigan: Inter-Varsity Press; Zondervan Pub. House , 2004), 317.

[20] Wayne A. Grudem, *Systematic Theology: An Introduction to Biblical Doctrine* (Leicester, England; Grand Rapids, Michigan: Inter-Varsity Press; Zondervan Pub. House , 2004), 319.

[21] Wayne A. Grudem, *Systematic Theology: An Introduction to Biblical Doctrine* (Leicester, England; Grand Rapids, Michigan: Inter-Varsity Press; Zondervan Pub. House , 2004), 322-23.

[22] Wayne A. Grudem, *Systematic Theology: An Introduction to Biblical Doctrine* (Leicester, England; Grand Rapids, Michigan: Inter-Varsity Press; Zondervan Pub. House , 2004), 338.

www.ingramcontent.com/pod-product-compliance
Lightning Source LLC
Chambersburg PA
CBHW060016050426
42448CB00012B/2772